Philosophy &Public Affairs

SUMMER 1991   VOLUME 20   NUMBER 3

Notes on
the Contributors

ANTHONY LADEN is a graduate student in philosophy at Harvard University.

ROSALIND HURSTHOUSE is Senior Lecturer in Philosophy at The Open University, England. Her recent articles include "Arational Actions" (*Journal of Philosophy*, February 1991) and "After Hume's Justice" (forthcoming in *Proceedings of the Aristotelian Society*, 1990–1991), which explores a neo-Aristotelian account of rights.

LYNN SHARP PAINE is Associate Professor at the Harvard Business School and a 1990–1991 Fellow in Harvard's Program in Ethics and the Professions. She has published a number of articles in the area of business ethics on topics such as competitive fairness, the ethics of competitor information gathering, and conflicts between work and family obligations. Her current research focuses on ethical and legal dimensions of the management of information and ideas.

ALAN GIBBARD is Professor of Philosophy at the University of Michigan, Ann Arbor. He is author of *Wise Choices, Apt Feelings: A Theory of Normative Judgment* (Harvard University Press, 1990).

ANTHONY LADEN

Games, Fairness, and Rawls's *A Theory of Justice*

There are few disciplines where game theorists fear to tread. They have rushed in with their mathematical analyses and attempted to formalize the thinking in fields as varied as economics and evolution. And in many cases their fresh, more formal approach has added clarity and insight to a less rigorous field. In other cases, however, forced to rely on simplifying assumptions in order to model any real behavior as a game, they have misunderstood the very concepts they have attempted to describe.

Political philosophy has not been free from such intrusions. In particular, contractualist theories such as that of John Rawls have seemed especially ripe for game-theoretic plucking. Unfortunately, much of this modeling has been done without a thorough understanding of the theories themselves, and the will to model has often lost sight of central philosophical concerns not captured by the theorist's game.

This article is an effort to rectify that situation at several levels. At the most basic level, I offer a sympathetic game-theoretic reading of Rawls's theory of justice as fairness that, I believe, captures many of the insights of that theory that other formal accounts have missed.[1] At a slightly more

This article is a descendant of a part of my B.A. honors thesis submitted to the Department of Philosophy at Harvard University in the spring of 1989. Much of the revision was done during a year spent at Corpus Christi College, Oxford, where I was supported by a Frank Knox Fellowship from Harvard and an Overseas Research Scholarship from the British government. I am enormously indebted to Amartya Sen, Susan Hurley, John Rawls, and Thomas Scanlon for many helpful discussions and suggestions. I would also like to thank Michael Bacharach, Ken Binmore, Robert Nozick, Kenneth Shepsle, Andrew Williams, and the Editors of *Philosophy & Public Affairs* for their helpful comments on earlier drafts.

1. Three such accounts are Ken Binmore, "Game Theory and the Social Contract, Mark II," ST/ICERD discussion paper 88/170 (London School of Economics and the University of Michigan, 1988; photocopied), and "Social Contract I: Rawls and Harsanyi," *Economic*

general level, the theory of fairness described in Section I of this article that motivates the reading of Rawls in Section II may be found to have more general application than I describe here. At first glance, for instance, it appears to be applicable to David Gauthier's account of morality.[2] Finally, at the most general level, I hope that this article as a whole will be seen as an example of what I take to be the proper way to use game theory in political philosophy.

In order to distinguish these three levels a little further, I will make some broad comments about each one before plunging into the arguments themselves. Political philosophy is an abstract and somewhat formal discipline, but its subject matter remains far more complex and subtly shaded than any game-theoretic model. As a result, when game theorists model political situations or philosophical accounts of them, they are prone to simplify, and, unfortunately, to misunderstand. Of course, game theorists are no more prone to misunderstand philosophers than anyone else, including other philosophers. What makes the game-theoretic misreadings so worrisome is the way they are subsequently cemented into mathematical rigor and thus rigidity. Plugging a misunderstanding into a mathematical model not only fails to clear up the misunderstanding, it locks it into place, disguising it in the formal attire of mathematics. But good philosophy is supple in a way that the relatively simple mathematics of game theory can never be. So game-theoretic accounts that misconstrue arguments not only misrepresent the substance, they also destroy the form of those ideas.

The literature on Rawls is replete with examples of this. Rawls's "original position" argument seems on the surface to be a game theorist's dream. Many critics approaching justice as fairness from a mathematical

---

Journal 99 (1989): 84–102; John Harsanyi, "Can the Maximin Principle Serve as the Basis for Morality?" *American Political Science Review* 69 (1975): 594–606; and Roger Howe and John Roemer, "Rawlsian Justice as the Core of a Game," *American Economic Review* 71 (1981): 880–95. Briefly, Binmore fails to take full account of Rawls's explicit concern with stability and thus models the original position in such a way as to make commitment an issue. Harsanyi treats justice as fairness as if it were trying to solve a question of allocative rather than distributive justice. In addition, he models the original position as a decision problem, not a game. Howe and Roemer collapse primary goods into income, which they then see as one argument of a utility function. Furthermore, they do not discuss the stability argument and thus conclude that the parties must be extremely risk averse in the original position. Such brief comments do not do justice to these authors, but more detailed and worthy criticisms are precluded here by space limitations.

2. See David Gauthier, *Morals by Agreement* (Oxford: Clarendon Press, 1986).

perspective focus exclusively on the choice of the principles from the original position and the use of maximin reasoning to arrive at the difference principle, and ignore the complexities of his arguments about stability and his concerns with fairness and reciprocity.

In order to avoid such mistakes, I will try to use game theory to gain a new vantage point and then, having done so, to rely not so much on its formalism as on the spirit of its arguments. Thus, instead of building a full-fledged game-theoretic model of the original position, throwing about some equations, and thus deriving the two principles of justice, I will suggest various analogies between forms of argument in the game-theoretic context and the Rawlsian case.

Of course, if philosophers can object that game theorists often sacrifice subtlety, game theorists can accuse philosophers of sacrificing precision. In order to avoid such a charge, I will present the theory of fairness in strictly game-theoretic terms. By not muddying the waters of game theory with philosophy in the first part of the article, I hope also to give the theory that I am advancing a somewhat broader scope.

Finally, it may help to provide, without the game theory, an overview of the picture of Rawls that the argument as a whole attempts to sketch. Essentially, the argument attempts to show that the contractualist argument from the original position that Rawls makes in support of the two principles of justice is much closer to Thomas Scanlon's contractualism[3] than it might appear at first glance. Scanlon's contractualism operates at a metaethical level and suggests that morally right principles are ones that "no one could reasonably reject." The difference between this account and Rawls's, then, appears to be that Scanlon requires that we check with everyone in order to ratify a set of principles, while Rawls only asks us to check with abstract individuals who represent everyone by having the contingent features of no one. Scanlon's position would thus be more sensitive to the special needs of specific groups in society whose determining characteristics would be abstracted away by the veil of ignorance. If it more easily took into account the diverse claims made by women, ethnic minorities, the handicapped, and so forth, it would also be a more appealing notion on which to ground a theory of justice.

I want to argue that these two theories are best seen as complemen-

---

3. See T. M. Scanlon, "Contractualism and Utilitarianism," in *Utilitarianism and Beyond,* ed. Amartya Sen and Bernard Williams (Cambridge: Cambridge University Press, 1982), pp. 103–28.

tary. Reading Rawls's theory as fundamentally like Scanlon's brings out the richness of his theory, by making clear how justice as fairness captures the full, diverse appeal of philosophical contractualism. Likewise, reading Scanlon's theory as so related to justice as fairness shows that it can be fleshed out in a more robust manner than he suggests.[4] Scanlon suggests a reading of justice as fairness that will bring it "closer to" his own theory,[5] and my argument can be seen as an attempt to bring them all the way together.[6] One of the consequences of taking these two theories as related in this way is that the role of ethical assumptions in justice as fairness becomes clear. For, as we shall see, Scanlon's theory requires an assumption that people are "reasonable," that they have "the desire to find principles which others similarly motivated could not reasonably reject."[7] Such motivation falls somewhere between the ethics-free self-interest maximization of the parties in John Harsanyi's contractualist account of utilitarianism[8] and the kind of moral, other-regarding motivations that Rawls explicitly rejects as a basis for reasoning in the original position,[9] and thus a reading that stresses the reasonableness (in Scanlon's sense) of the parties in the original position will serve to show Rawls's description of that position and the parties therein as richer and less mechanical than it is often taken to be.

To see how justice as fairness captures Scanlon's conception, it is necessary to recall that the argument from the original position has two parts. In the first and more familiar part, principles are chosen from a list of alternatives by parties in an original position behind a veil of ignorance. From the perspective of the original position, Rawls singles out particular principles of justice. But it is not until the second stage that he advances many of the arguments that bear the weight of justifying those principles. The second part of the argument focuses on the stabil-

---

4. Ibid., p. 127.

5. Ibid., p. 124 n. 19.

6. This remark is not meant to deny the obvious difference between the two theories. Scanlon's theory is clearly meant to be a broad account of ethical motivation, whereas Rawls considers his theory to be a narrowly political conception of justice. They still apply to overlapping terrains, however, and it is to this overlap that my argument is meant to apply.

7. Scanlon, "Contractualism and Utilitarianism," p. 116 n. 12.

8. See, e.g., Harsanyi, "Can the Maximin Principle Serve?"

9. John Rawls, *A Theory of Justice* (Cambridge, Mass.: Harvard University Press, 1971), pp. 142–44.

ity of a society that is well ordered by the principles selected in the first
part. Here, the parties "consider the special psychologies by checking
whether those who grow up under just institutions (as the principles
adopted specify them) will develop a sufficiently firm sense of justice
with respect to those attitudes and inclinations."[10]

It is in this second part of the argument that Rawls bridges the gap
between what many critics have taken him to be saying and Scanlon's
position. By treating philosophical contractualism as an account of fairness and analyzing it in game-theoretic terms, we will find a very strong
link between the type of fairness Scanlon describes and the type of stability Rawls insists that his principles produce. Thus, the very fact that
Rawls requires his chosen principles to be stable and argues at great
length that they are demonstrates that the fairness he wants to capture
through the device of the original position is similar to that captured by
Scanlon's theory. Understanding the fundamental roles that stability and
fairness play in Rawls's theory will allow us to see the first part of his
argument, the part about the original position, in a new light as well.
Instead of merely seeing an abstract choice problem, we will be able to
understand better the way various characteristics of the original position,
such as its symmetry and the veil of ignorance, are meant to capture
some notion of the reasonable as well.

I should make clear at this point that I do not think that the only way
to come to this understanding of justice as fairness is through the game-
theoretic route I take here. There are many routes to this vantage point,
some of which appear in the literature.[11] The advantages of taking the
route via game theory seem to me to be two. First, game theorists have
some of the most strident voices advocating a reading of Rawls focusing
on caution and maximin reasoning. Thus, showing that one can come to
the understanding of Rawls that I do here through game theory goes
some way toward undermining these critics. Second, by trying to capture
various features of Rawls's complex structure in a simple formal model,
we may be able to see more clearly how and whether the picture hangs

10. John Rawls, "Justice as Fairness: A Brief Restatement" (Harvard University, 1990;
photocopied), sec. 55, p. 153.
11. See, e.g., Edward F. McClennen, "Justice and the Problem of Stability," *Philosophy
& Public Affairs* 18, no. 1 (Winter 1989): 3–30, and Joshua Cohen, "Democratic Equality,"
Ethics 99 (1989): 727–51.

together in ways that might be obscured by the size and detail of the theory as a whole.

I. Games and Fairness

When we maintain that a given procedure is not fair, we claim to have a legitimate complaint against that procedure. Generally, the type of complaint we describe as an allegation of the unfairness of a procedure is not contingent upon the plaintiff's place in the final outcome. An undesirable outcome might give rise to a complaint of unfairness, or move us to examine the fairness of the procedure more closely. If we are arguing against unfairness, however, we will want to make a more general argument than "I wanted more."

A fairness argument also carries some moral weight. When we say we were treated unfairly, we are saying that we ought to have been treated differently and, in our view, better. In some way or another we did not receive the treatment we were entitled to under some broader category of rules.

Finally, fairness criteria must satisfy what Rawls calls a generality condition.[12] That is, fair conditions cannot use particular names as rigid designators. The consequence of this condition is that there is no moral distinction between calling something unfair and calling it unfair to a specific person or group or class of persons, for if a principle is unfair to a subset of the population, then it is unfair, period. The need for generality, then, requires special attention to those who fare particularly badly under a given process, for they are the people most likely to have been treated unfairly.

While fairness is a complex notion, and the boundaries between what is fair and unfair are fuzzy, there would seem to be certain procedures and games that we can all agree are fair. In general, reasons for calling a given game fair do not conflict; if two people disagree as to whether a game is fair, the extra restrictions that must be added to satisfy the doubter will rarely make the believer question the fairness of the revised game. Thus, to satisfy everyone that a game is fair, we begin by designing a game that we think is indisputably fair, and then add further rules that will satisfy more and more people that the game is fair.[13]

12. Rawls, *A Theory of Justice*, p. 131.

13. This claim is tendentious, and deserves more discussion than I give it here. The

*Games, Fairness, and
Rawls's* A Theory
of Justice

The definition of fairness that I offer below relies on our ability to agree at first glance that some group of games are fair, and attempts to push out the boundaries of what we are willing to call fair by offering an iterative function that preserves fairness. The function maps games to subsets of their cores, a notion that will be discussed later. If a particular game is in the transitive closure of this function applied to an indisputably fair game, then it will be fair. Owing to the structure of the definition, we will have two types of fairness. The first, "intrinsic fairness," will apply to the indisputably fair games to which we apply the fairness-preserving function initially. The second, "derived fairness," will be a property of games that are the result of applying the function to fair games. Before providing a full mathematical statement of the theory and its proof, it will help to discuss the philosophical ideas on which it is based and the mathematical concepts it invokes. We will start with the philosophy.

As I mentioned previously, Scanlon's contractualism captures a rather rich concept of fairness, which should be clear from the intuitive remarks already made. Scanlon feels that contractualist ethics captures the main motivating force behind ethical claims: our wish to be able to justify the principles by which we live to those with whom we live. Thus, people in all positions will appeal to the sorts of arguments he describes to dispute the morality of a given set of principles. Not only the badly off have an interest in fairness. Even those who do well under given procedures and principles have an interest in defending them as fair, and thus arguing that they are entitled to their well-being, that they got what they have fair and square. This fits in with our idea that fairness should be a general concept, related to procedures and principles, not individual outcomes directly. Finally, Scanlon offers criteria that are at least jointly sufficient for rejectability. To the extent that these can be formalized, they will provide a check that a mathematical account of fairness is on the mark.

---

point of making such an argument is to ground the theory that follows. That theory requires that there be indisputably fair games, and this argument, if it goes through, would guarantee such games. If it turns out that indisputably fair games do not exist, however, that would seem to undermine the entire project of basing justice on fairness in order to secure common consent. And if that were the case, Rawlsian liberalism would be in trouble for reasons far more complex than those I am discussing here. Thus I will continue assuming that there exists an indisputably fair game from which the relevant justice games could be derived.

The other philosophical concept that provides support for this definition is John Roemer's game-theoretic definition of exploitation.[14] Roemer
links exploitation to the cores of games, showing that the cores of games
provide nonexploitative allocations within a given society.[15] The fact that
the cores of games are nonexploitative provides grounds for believing
that the outcomes in the core will not be unfair either. In order to understand why outcomes in the core will preserve the fairness of the games
of which they are the result, however, it is necessary to discuss the core
and various other game-theoretic notions related to it.

The core is an equilibrium of a cooperative game. Cooperative games
are defined as those in which the players are allowed to communicate
with one another and thus form coalitions based on binding agreements.
As a result, cooperative games have to be characterized not only by the
options open to individuals, but also by the options open to coalitions,
defined as any subset S of the full player set N. Coalition strength is
measured by a characteristic function, $v(S)$, which maps the set of all
coalitions to the payoffs they can guarantee themselves. Thus, we can
define a cooperative game by its player set and its characteristic function.[16]

The final outcome of a given game (cooperative or not) is called an
imputation, and is denoted by the n-dimensional vector **x**. An imputation
merely says which of the n individuals of the player set gets what. For
an imputation to be a plausible outcome of a cooperative game, three
conditions must be met. First, it must be individually rational: all players
must receive at least what they could get if they were to play on their

14. John Roemer, *A General Theory of Exploitation and Class* (Cambridge, Mass.: Harvard University Press, 1982), p. 197.

15. See ibid., p. 198, for proof.

16. It is sometimes thought that the notion of a characteristic function is on shaky
ground philosophically because it refers to what a coalition can achieve apart from the
actions of the rest of the players. To avoid this problem, note that there are two ways to
construct a characteristic function. The first of these relies on the one action a coalition
may take without regard for other players: quit the game. If a coalition can withdraw from
a game, take all its marbles and go home, then the amount with which it can leave (the
value of its marbles, as it were) is the value of the characteristic function for that coalition.
The second relies on maximin strategies and thus does not involve any unilateral action on
the part of the coalition in question. Any set of jointly performed strategies will have a worst
possible outcome. If the coalition plays the joint strategy with the highest worst payoff
(maximizing its minimum), then we say it plays its maximin strategy. Clearly, any coalition
can guarantee itself its maximin payoff, and thus it can be used as the value of a characteristic function as well. Both of these methods of construction will come up below.

own. Mathematically, we have, for each i, $x_i \geq v(i)$. Second, the imputation must be collectively rational: the sum of the distributions must be the same as what the grand coalition N (the coalition of all n players) can guarantee itself, that is, the total amount available in the game. This requirement is equivalent to saying that the distribution is Pareto-optimal.

Finally, the imputation must satisfy coalitional rationality. This condition stipulates that evey coalition receives at least as much as it is guaranteed by the characteristic function. If we denote the amount a coalition S receives from the imputation **x** as $x(S)$, then coalitional rationality requires that for all S, $x(S) \geq v(S)$. Imputations that satisfy this condition for all coalitions are said to be in the core of the game. Note that if a coalition receives at least as much as it is guaranteed, it will have no incentive to break away from the grand coalition. Thus, imputations in the core are stable, as there is no group of players who can act collectively in such a way as to improve their lot.

While the core has come to be the standard equilibrium concept in the theory of cooperative games, it does have two significant drawbacks. Many games do not have cores, and in those that do have cores, the core is often not a unique imputation. The first fact, on its own, does not invalidate the core as an apt criterion for fairness. Fairness is a desirable property, and it should come as no surprise that most systems of rules are not fair. If every game had a core, then the core would not provide a suitable description of fairness, for all games would then be fair.

Lack of uniqueness is, on its own, not a problem either. If all outcomes in the core turn out to be equally fair, then it will not matter which one is chosen, at least as far as fairness is concerned. Nevertheless, it will sometimes be possible to differentiate between outcomes in the core in terms of fairness. Since we can talk of systems as being more and less fair as well as being absolutely fair or unfair outside of the models of game theory, we want a formal definition of fairness to be able to capture these finer distinctions. To see how some outcomes in the core might be fairer than others, it is important to see why games have cores at all.

Games in which the subcoalitions are relatively weak compared to the grand coalition are likely to have cores. If the subcoalitions are weak, it will be possible for them to merge with other coalitions and still get their guaranteed per capita payoffs even though the total payoff to the larger merged coalition is being divided into more parts. Thus, in games that do have cores, there will often be a surplus payoff to the grand coalition that can be divided in a number of ways while still meeting every coalition's guaranteed payoff. The problem of choosing between different imputations in the core of a game, then, will resemble the problem of how to distribute any productive surplus. What we need is a way of ranking various imputations in the core of a given game in terms of their fairness.

In order to do so, however, we need a little more machinery. The first tool we need is the *excess*. The excess a coalition S receives from an imputation $\mathbf{x}$, denoted $e(\mathbf{x}, S)$, is the difference between what it could guarantee itself and what it receives. That is, $e(\mathbf{x}, S) = v(S) - x(S)$. Note that the excess is defined so that a negative excess is preferable to a positive one, and the more negative the better.

We can now redefine the core in terms of the excess as follows: Any imputation $\mathbf{x}$ is in the core if and only if, for all coalitions S, $e(\mathbf{x}, S) \leq 0$. Next, define the ϵ-core as the set of all imputations x satisfying $e(\mathbf{x}, S) \leq \epsilon$, for all coalitions S. In this terminology, the core is now the 0-core. Note that as we decrease ϵ, we get smaller and smaller sets. For some value of ϵ, the ϵ-core will be empty. Let the smallest value of ϵ for which there is a nonempty ϵ-core be ϵ'. Then the ϵ'-core is called the *least core* (LC).

Although ϵ-cores will allow us to make finer distinctions between procedures in our definition of fairness, they might be thought to have two significant drawbacks in terms of their applicability to philosophy. First, since most philosophical examples and theories do not rely explicitly on numbers, it will be hard to differentiate between the .5-core and the 1-core, for instance. Despite this problem, it will be possible to single out certain procedures as members of the least core in many situations, and so we can incorporate it directly into our definition of fairness without loss of applicability.

Second, the motivational arguments for the core are not effective for negative ϵ-cores. For one coalition to argue for a move from a position outside the core to one inside the core, all it needs to do is threaten to withdraw. Since, with an outcome outside the core, it is not receiving its guaranteed payoff, such a threat is credible; the coalition has an incentive to leave. Such an argument fails to work with negative ϵ-cores. For instance, if an outcome is in the core but not the least core, then a coalition that would do better in the least core cannot make the same sort of credible threat to withdraw, because they are already doing at least as well as they were guaranteed. Since carrying out the threat of withdrawal would leave them worse off than they are, it appears unlikely that such a threat would sway the other players to give up their surplus in order to move to the least core. There is an argument that can be made, but it is one that relies on the broader context in which the game is played, more ethical concerns, and arguments about the relations between the players and not just how one player or coalition does alone. To move from the core to the least core, a coalition S might claim that the outcome in the least core would be better for it and, in addition, no one else would be as badly off as S is now. Such an argument might have motivating force if other games are to be played and thus it is important to foster good will, or because the other players are concerned to be fair or just. For now, however, I only want to point out that the arguments for positions in the least core when ϵ is negative will be of a very different character from those that go only as far as the core, primarily in that they rely on relations between coalitions and strong conceptions of reciprocity. It is in these types of arguments that we will see the ethical force of Scanlon's assumption of reasonableness come into the theory.

At this point I want to return to Scanlon's theory and begin to sketch a formal definition of fairness. The point of doing this is to attempt to formalize his conditions for rejectability in order to more easily compare his theory with Rawls's. Although Scanlon does not provide a formal account of when something is fair, he does provide two grounds for rejectability that he regards as at least jointly sufficient: "if (1) general acceptance of that principle in a world like the one we are familiar with would cause that person serious hardship, and (2) there are alternative principles general acceptance of which would not entail comparable burdens for anyone."[17]

With these grounds in hand, formalization is rather straightforward once we add an obvious generalization to Scanlon's conditions. If there is no individual who can reasonably reject a principle, then there will be no reason for any group of people to reject it. Clearly, if any group can reject a principle, then any individual member of that group can reject it on the same grounds. Thus, these conditions for rejectability will satisfy both individual and coalitional rationality. In game-theoretic terms, prin-

17. T. M. Scanlon, "Value, Desire, and the Quality of Life," in *The Quality of Life,* ed. Martha Nussbaum and Amartya Sen (New York: Oxford University Press, 1991).

ciples that lead to imputations in the core of a game are not rejectable. We need, however, to tailor this thought to make it fully compatible with our notions of fairness and with Scanlon's notion of reasonableness. While we might not have any reason for rejecting an outcome in the core of a game *once we have agreed to play that game,* in order for us to say that a given outcome in the core is fair, we will need to say more about the game itself. Specifically, we should have no reason to reject playing the game in the first place. The division between the rejectability of games and the rejectability of their noncore outcomes will line up to some degree with Scanlon's two conditions. The first stage rules out games that inevitably lead to serious hardship, and once we agree to play a game, the second condition will be fulfilled by players who are reasonable in Scanlon's sense of the term. Putting these two criteria together— fair games have fair cores—we can develop an iterative definition of fairness based on the cores of games.

Before doing so, I want to introduce a piece of terminology that is not standard in most treatments of game theory. Define a *metagame* as a game whose outcomes are other games. In game theory parlance, this is most similar to the first moves of a supergame, where a supergame is a large game made up of smaller games played in successive stages. I use the term metagame to emphasize the separateness of the games involved. An example of a metagame is a sports league. Here, two games are often played to determine a champion. The first is called "the regular season," and the outcome of this game is a second game, called "the playoffs." By playing the regular season, the league selects which playoff game it will play, that is, which teams, in which order, and at which stadia. Thus, the regular season is a metagame, while the playoffs, which terminate with a given champion, are a game in the normal sense.

Another example, relevant to political philosophy, is Rawls's four-stage sequence.[18] According to Rawls, parties in the original position pick principles to govern the basic structure. These principles define a particular constitutional convention where rules will be chosen, which will then determine the nature of the legislature. The legislature, in turn, enacts specific laws. Finally, these laws determine the way a judiciary rules in specific cases. If we think of this as a series of nested metagames, we can say that the parties in the original position play a metagame in which

18. Rawls, *A Theory of Justice,* pp. 195–96.

they choose what constitutional metagame that society will play, the representatives at the convention play a metagame to determine which legislative metagame will be played, and so on.

With the notion of a metagame in hand, we can now define a fair game as follows. A game G is fair if and only if there is a series of metagames G_o, G_1, . . . G_n such that each has a nonempty core, G_o is indisputably fair, each G_i is in the least core of G_{i-1}, and G is in the least core of G_n. Since there will be many indisputably fair games, we will have many such series, but as long as we can trace a game's pedigree back through a series of least cores to a fair metagame, we will be able to say that it is fair.

Note that this procedure will produce games that meet the highest criteria of fairness. In many cases, it may be enough to stipulate that each G_i be in the core of G_{i-1}—at worst this will produce games that might be characterized as "not unfair."

One question left open at this stage is precisely how the players in a metagame are to evaluate the outcome games. In terms of the formal structure of game theory, they will need to be able to do so on some single, cardinal metric if excesses and ϵ-cores are to be used. There are several plausible ways of constructing such a metric, and which one is used will depend primarily on the situation to which the definition is to be applied. We might imagine that the players work out how the successive games will be played until they reach a determinate payoff and then work backward to evaluate the games at hand. Another method would be for them to assign expected utility values to each of the outcome games. Whatever method of evaluation we choose, however, will have to distinguish between three forms of fairness. I have already pointed out the distinction between intrinsic and derived fairness. The third form of fairness comes from making a further distinction between the derived fairness of metagames and the derived fairness of standard games, those with standard payoffs in dollars, utils, bundles of goods, or whatever. The first and last of these forms of fairness are the easiest to grasp. Intrinsic fairness is independent of cores and least cores, and is due to such considerations as symmetry and whether players who are similar in the relevant respects are treated similarly. The derived fairness of standard games is purely a property of their outcomes. Since these are ordinary payoffs, we can calculate cores and least cores in the regular fashion.

The trouble arises when we try to flesh out the notion of the core or least core of a metagame. If our method of evaluation fails to distinguish between the evaluation of metagames and the evaluation of standard games, we are likely to evaluate metagames by tracing through a sequence of games from the metagame to a final regular game and then evaluating the metagame in terms of the payoffs in the standard game. Although in some cases, collapsing metagames into standard games in this fashion may be the proper way to make evaluations, doing so as a matter of course will forfeit much of the richness the theory of fairness gets from its use of metagames. In the case of Rawls's view, it will confuse allocative and distributive justice.

How, then, are we to evaluate metagames and argue whether or not their outcome games are in the core or least core? In many cases we will have to rely on analogies and close examination of the types of arguments coalitions can make about the desirability of playing or not playing a given outcome game. I realize that at this stage, such a formulation is highly suspect and none too clear. A thorough application of this notion will be presented in my discussion of Rawls in Section II.

While a more technical proof than the one offered below can be constructed, the following argument should provide an adequate case for why this definition of fairness and Scanlon's two criteria for rejectability carve out the same space. It will also shed some light on the type of arguments the players of a game make in order to arrive at an outcome in either the core or the least core.

I want to show that a game G satisfies the above conditions if and only if we cannot reasonably reject it. To do so, I will show that the contrapositives hold; that is, that if a game does not satisfy them then we can reasonably reject it as unfair, and that if we can reasonably reject it, then the required series of metagames does not exist.

To show that if a game is not in the least core then we can reasonably reject it, I proceed in two stages: If an imputation is not in the core (and thus not in the least core), then it gives a coalition less than its maximin strategy would have yielded in the fair metagame. But, if it gives the coalition less than it could guarantee on its own, and so less than it was sure of receiving when it agreed to play the game, the coalition has reasonable though purely self-interested grounds for rejecting that imputation and thus the outcome game it represents. As I mentioned before, the nonrejectability of the metagame itself takes care of Scanlon's "serious hardship" condition. In addition, the fairness of the characteristic

function of the metagame serves to limit the types of claims that can be
made here. There is no room for someone to make just any claim that
she could do better on her own. Thus, for instance, the fact that Robert
Nozick's Wilt Chamberlain[19] might make more money by dropping out
of society and charging people to watch him play basketball than he does
in a certain imputation of a fair game does not necessarily give him the
ability to reject that imputation. The notion of *doing better* is defined
here solely in terms of the characteristic function (so Chamberlain has a
claim only if the imputation in question gives him less than the characteristic function of this game he has already agreed to play does), and so
the significance of being able to do better in this nonrejectable game is
that the final outcome is reasonably rejectable.

At the second stage, we look at imputations in the core, but not the
least core. If **x** is such an imputation, then a coalition could reject it with
the following argument: There is another imputation, **y**, also in the core,
which does better for the coalition, and which does not treat any other
group as badly as it is treated by **x**. That is, the coalition could invoke
Scanlon's second condition for rejectability. It is worth noting that this
argument would be sufficient on its own for rejecting any imputation not
in the least core, whether or not it was also in the core. That would seem
to imply that in cases of fairness at least, Scanlon's second condition
would be sufficient on its own to guarantee nonrejectability. Once again,
we are assuming that the game itself is not rejectable, and so to the extent that Scanlon's first condition enters into the picture here, it enters
in with this assumption. To understand why there will always be a coalition that can appeal to an appropriate **y**, it will help to look at an example. Take a game where the least core is the -2-core. Then, for **x** to be
in the core of the game, but not in the least core, there must be a coalition S such that $-2 < e(\mathbf{x}, S) \leq 0$. Now, not only is it the case that an
imputation **y** in the least core will be better for S, but, in addition, there
will not be any other coalition that does as badly under **y** as S does under
x.

By breaking up the first half of the argument into two points, we can
see clearly the added degree of fairness brought in by a reliance on least
cores instead of standard cores as well as the different natures of the

19. See Robert Nozick, *Anarchy, State and Utopia* (New York: Basic Books, 1974), pp.
161–63.

arguments that reject noncore and non-least-core outcomes. The argument that rejects imputations not in the core relies on a notion of reciprocity based on mutual advantage relative to what coalitions can achieve on their own. It requires a consideration of only how well that coalition does and what it was guaranteed by the game it had already agreed to play. The arguments rejecting imputations in the core rely on a stronger notion of reciprocity, one that requires consideration of the relationships between different coalitions. Specifically, it requires that the better-off not benefit at the expense of the worse-off, since moving away from the least core amounts to taking from the worse-off and giving to the better-off. As it was Scanlon's second condition that provided the motivation for making this sort of argument, we can see here the affinity between Scanlon's notion of reasonableness and questions of reciprocity. Later we will see how these questions of reciprocity are central to Rawls's argument.

It is worth reiterating the relation between the various two-step procedures floating around at this stage. Specifically, the two steps in the first half of the proof do not match up with Scanlon's two conditions for rejectability. His first condition is taken care of by the fairness of the game in question, while the second condition is being addressed in both steps of the preceding proof. The purpose of doing the proof in two steps is to show the added degree of fairness that comes in with the least core instead of the core, and to distinguish two types of arguments against lack of fairness that can be made. When we turn to Rawls, we will see that this division lines up with the division between his two principles of justice, and the arguments he now makes in support of them.

To show that if a game is rejectable then there is no series of nested metagames that connect it to an indisputably fair metagame, we proceed by contradiction. Assume that we have reasonable grounds for rejecting some outcome x, and that x is in the least core of some metagame G_n that has a nonempty core, which is an outcome of another metagame G_{n-1}. Let this nesting continue back to G_o, which is indisputably fair. Let us further assume that x is the worst possible outcome there is for us in the least core of G_n. Then x must be at least as good as the outcome guaranteed by our maximin strategy, for otherwise it would give us less than we could guarantee on our own, and thus would not even be in the core. If, however, we can reasonably reject x, for whatever reason, we certainly have grounds for rejecting an outcome that gives us less than

x. Thus, we have grounds for rejecting our maximin guarantee. If, however, we can reasonably reject our guaranteed outcome, we have
grounds for reasonably rejecting the game G_n in the first place. Arguing
inductively backward, we can now ask, why can we reasonably reject G_n
if it is in the least core of G_{n-1}? At some point we must find a G_i that is
not in the core of G_{i-1}, or we must be able to reject G_o, either of which
contradicts our hypothesis, and this completes the proof.

Before proceeding to a discussion of Rawls, let me make two conceptual points. First, why should we expect that fair games, in general, have
cores, quite apart from this theory? Imagine a fair game G with an empty
core. Then for any imputation **x** in G, there will be some coalition S for
which $x(S) < v(S)$. (If there were no such S, then **x** would be in the core.)
Since the game must at least be additive,[20] we know that $v(N) \geq v(N-S)$
$+ v(S)$. And since **x** must satisfy collective rationality, $x(N-S) + x(S)$
$= v(N)$. From these facts, it follows that $x(N-S) > v(N-S)$. Thus, no
matter how the game turns out, some will gain at the expense of others,
as given by v. Since the outcomes are other games, some of the players
of the next game will start from a weaker position. Now, look at the situation from the point of view of the outcome game alone. Some players
come into the game with an advantage over others that is greater than it
otherwise would have been for no apparent reason. Clearly, such a game
will be unfair. Since the original game necessarily leads to a second
game that is not fair, the original game cannot be said to be fair either.
Thus, the core cannot be empty if the game is to be fair.

Second, since the core is a concept in the theory of cooperative games,
this definition will only apply to cooperative games. In particular, prisoner's dilemmas, games like chess, and, in fact, two-person games in general will not be covered by this definition. This is not to pass judgment
on these sorts of games, but only to point out that they do not fall under
the jurisdiction of the theory advanced above.

II. RAWLS AND FAIRNESS

With a game-theoretic description of fairness in hand, I now turn to
Rawls's theory and show how a game-theoretic approach from fairness

20. A game is additive if for all coalitions S and T, $v(S \cup T) = v(S) + v(T)$.

provides a new perspective from which to view justice as fairness as a whole.

The argument for the two principles of justice from the original position is divided roughly into two parts. The first part deals with the choice of the two principles from a list of known and viable alternatives behind the veil of ignorance. While the mere fact that a set of principles would be chosen at this stage is enough to imbue those principles with a certain moral distinction, Rawls does not claim that this alone justifies them as a set of principles of justice that can regulate the basic structure of society. He is explicit on this point, noting that "the argument for the principles of justice is not complete until the principles selected in the first part are shown in the second part to be sufficiently stable. So in *Theory* the argument is not complete until the next to last section."[21]

However, the second part, which contains an argument that the two principles of justice would be stable for a well-ordered society, is necessary to validate the principles chosen by the parties in the original position. If the argument for stability fails, so must the entire conception of justice. The reason for this may surprise those critics of the original position who find its conception of human nature too barren or fictitious to be usable. As Rawls explains, the argument about stability is an attempt to check whether the assumptions made in the formulation of the original position were correct. He must show that they work and are not unreasonable: "The essential advantage of the two-step procedure is that no particular constellation of attitudes is taken as given. We are simply checking the reasonableness of our initial assumptions and the consequences we have drawn from them in the light of the constraints imposed by the general facts of the world."[22]

Despite Rawls's insistence on the importance of the second part of the argument for the two principles of justice, most commentators, especially those approaching Rawls from a game-theoretic perspective, downplay or completely ignore this part of the argument.[23] But without a suf-

21. John Rawls, "The Domain of the Political and Overlapping Consensus," *New York University Law Review* 64 (1989): 245 n. 27. See also Rawls, *A Theory of Justice*, pp. 144, 530–31.

22. Rawls, *A Theory of Justice*, p. 531.

23. Two recent notable exceptions to this are McClennen, "Problem of Stability," and Cohen, "Democratic Equality." McClennen argues for the two principles of justice by discarding the original position, adding in certain communitarian concerns, and relying on Rawls's arguments for stability to bear the main weight of the theory. While his approach

ficient understanding of the role, or even the existence, of this second part, any game-theoretic analysis (in fact, any analysis at all) is bound to misrepresent justice as fairness. Such readings are bound to put too much weight on the first part of the argument from the original position.

There are two consequences of taking both parts of Rawls's argument seriously in a game-theoretic account of justice as fairness. The first is that the original position needs to be modeled not as one but as two games. The second is that the concepts of fairness and stability have to be analyzed in terms of the structure of the two original position games. When the latter is done, we will find a strong connection between the arguments from fairness and the arguments for stability. This connection provides the structural support for Rawls's conception of justice that many game-theoretic critics have found lacking in the original position as they construe it.

I should point out at this stage a somewhat paradoxical feature of my analysis. Treating the original position as a game (or even two games) makes it easier to think of it as a real situation in which people retreat to some sort of amnesia-inducing philosophical back room in order to make decisions about society. Such a picture, however, misrepresents what the original position is designed to do in the argument as a whole. It is meant to help us think clearly about the restrictions it seems reasonable to place on the sorts of arguments that can be made in favor of one set of principles of justice over another. Many of the mistakes that game theorists and others make in discussing Rawls can be traced to this sort of misunderstanding, and the fact that I am analyzing the original position in game-theoretic terms makes it crucial to emphasize that I am treating the original position in the latter, nonreified fashion.

A related point can be made about the similarity between the least core and the difference principle. In a symmetrical game in which everyone starts with nothing, the least core will be the maximin allocation (the one that makes the worst-off best off). Thus, it may be thought that a definition of fairness that requires players to choose strategies so as to arrive

---

differs from mine in ignoring the original position altogether and thus denying the strong link between fairness and stability that I am asserting, our two perspectives are parallel in many ways, and readers interested in a more thorough summary of Rawls's argument for stability would do well to look at the opening sections of his article. Cohen argues for a Scanlonian reading of Rawls very similar to mine, although minus the game-theoretic trappings. I find myself in particularly strong agreement with his concluding remarks.

at an outcome in the least core in order to preserve fairness will equate fairness and the difference principle by definition and thus support Rawls's position by sleight of hand. In order to see why my argument is not circular, let us distinguish between two levels at which it is operating. The first, more abstract level concerns games and fairness. At this level, as we have already seen, the fairest outcome game of a metagame will be one that is in the least core of the metagame. Players of the metagame concerned with issues of fairness will thus have added reasons to collectively use strategies leading to an outcome game in the least core. This is a general fact about games. At the applied level of the original position, it so happens that the two principles of justice are the only outcome in the least core of the original position game I will describe. That this is so requires a certain degree of argument, just as the conclusion that the parties in the original position will pick the two principles requires argument. Since the original position game will not have payoffs stipulated in primary goods, the two principles will not fall directly out of the game itself in the way a maximin allocation falls out of a symmetrical game as the least core. Recall the distinction I mentioned earlier between the evaluation of metagames and standard games. In a standard game, the units of the payoffs will be stipulated, but in the original position, the units are still under discussion. The parties might debate between a maximin allocation of utility and a maximin allocation of primary goods, and it is not clear on the face of it which of these would be in the least core of the metagame they are playing. In fact, it seems to me that in a slightly different game, in which the players were also asked to consider the two principles applied not to primary goods but to capabilities, it might be the case that Sen's principles and not Rawls's would form the least core of the game.[24] We are less likely to confuse these two levels if we think of the least core as the outcome of a certain strategy for playing a game, while we think of the difference principle as a principle for regulating a society rather than an allocative outcome.

24. For an account of capabilities and why they might be preferable to primary goods as an index of distributive justice, see Amartya Sen, "Justice: Means versus Freedoms," *Philosophy & Public Affairs* 19, no. 2 (Spring 1990): 111–21. It is unclear exactly how much difference there is between the two indices in practice, however, and to the extent that they are the same, my point is somewhat moot. If, however, there are significant differences between them, one might be able to make an argument for Sen's principles by showing that they were in the least core of an original position game in which they were on the list of principles to be considered.

This point about levels inevitably leads to questions about the units in which the parties in the original position games I shall describe evaluate different outcomes, which are just other games. Before discussing this, however, I want to make several other points about the original position, and begin to sketch out the two-game model I will propose.

One common—but, I shall argue, mistaken—method of modeling the original position is as a bargaining game with limited information. The limited information takes the place of the veil of ignorance, while the existence of many players and the bargaining structure account for the fact that the principles chosen will be applied to a society comprising many people with conflicting conceptions of the good. In order to accomplish the move from the choice of principles behind the veil to the application of those principles to society, some sort of lottery is invoked in which the parties in the original position are randomly assigned to their social positions. This sort of analysis leads to talk of members of society wanting to reenact the lottery if the principles are unsatisfactory to some, and the need for a commitment mechanism to prevent the parties from reneging on their agreement once they become people in the real world.[25] Such a model, however, does not accurately describe the Rawlsian original position, and creates many problems for the argument for justice as fairness that are not present in Rawls's account. Here it will suffice to note that if we keep in mind Rawls's assertion that the parties in the original position are to be regarded as "trustees" for the members of society, concerned to advance the interests of those they represent rather than to maximize their own well-being,[26] it will be less tempting to fall into talk of entrance lotteries.

At this point we need to ask why, if all of the parties in the original position are made identical by the veil of ignorance, we should think about it in game-theoretic as opposed to decision-theoretic terms. In order for game-theoretic reasoning to be appropriate, there must be some sort of strategic interaction between the parties in the original position; the results of the decisions they make must affect and be affected by the decisions made by others. There are several reasons to think this might be so despite the identical natures and situations of the parties. I will quickly mention these and then offer a model of the first part of the orig-

25. See, e.g., Binmore, "Game Theory" and "Social Contract I," and Howe and Roemer, "Rawlsian Justice."

26. Rawls, *A Theory of Justice*, p. 129.

inal position that is truly a game and, I believe, still captures the spirit of Rawls's description.

The main reason to think of it as a decision problem derives from the fact that the veil situates all of the parties identically, and so we can determine how all of them will reason by determining how any one of them will. But to say that this reduces the problem to a decision problem is to confuse symmetrical games with decision problems. In the prisoner's dilemma, for instance, we need only think how one of the prisoners will act to know how they both will act (in the abstract case, at least), but this does not make it any less of a game.

Looking at Rawls's description and use of the original position, we can find several reasons to think it ought to be treated as a true game. The first thing to note is Rawls's continued use of the plural in discussing the parties in the original position. His statement that "it is essential that the parties as rational representatives should be led to the *same* judgment as to which principles to accept"[27] can be read in this light. If the original position could be viewed as a pure decision problem, there would be no reason to stipulate that the parties come to unanimous agreement, just as there is no reason to insist that individuals make no more than one decision when faced with choices—they cannot do otherwise. Of course, this fact alone does not mean that the original position can be correctly thought of as a game. It certainly provides grounds for further investigation, however.

Second, it helps to remember that the reason for invoking the original position as a device is to bring notions of fairness into our arguments for justice. But fairness is, in general, a property of procedures that arrange interaction between competing interests, and so for the original position to capture a rich notion of fairness, it needs to be represented as a game and not a decision problem.

The final point I want to make regarding why the original position is best thought of as a game concerns Rawls's emphasis on publicity as both a formal constraint and a reason for choosing the difference principle.[28] The need for publicity arises because there are many people whose actions are interdependent; thus we find Rawls describing the publicity condition as requiring that "the parties in the original position, in evalu-

27. Rawls, "A Brief Restatement," sec. 25, p. 71 (italics mine).
28. Ibid., secs. 25 and 35. See also Rawls, *A Theory of Justice*, pp. 16, 175, 177–82.

ating principles, are to take into account the consequences, social and
psychological, of the public recognition by citizens that these principles
are mutually acknowledged and effectively regulate the basic structure."[29] We can think of the publicity requirement as analogous to a common knowledge requirement found in many games. Once again, common knowledge is a feature of games and not decision problems. The
final case for treating the original position as a game, however, must
come from the model itself. The preceding points provide ample reason
to believe that the original position cannot be adequately modeled as a
decision problem. The model that follows ought to provide ample evi-
dence that it can be accurately captured as a game.

In order to capture the two-step nature of Rawls's argument, and to
avoid the problems associated with lotteries, the model will describe the
original position as two games instead of one. The first game I call the
"choice game." It should be understood, however, that it is still a true
game. Its name arises from its function in the argument; in playing the
choice game, the parties make an initial choice of principles to regulate
the basic structure. In the choice game, the parties behind the veil attempt to make rational choices about which principles of justice will best
serve the interests of those they represent. The choice game works as
follows: Each of the n players is a trustee for a group of equal size in an
unknown society. They are unaware of the identity of those for whom
they are acting as trustees, or what the society these people live in is like
apart from the fact that it meets the requirements of justice. Each player
can choose a set of principles from a given list that will regulate the basic
structure of the society in which the people she represents will live. All
of the people represented by players who make the same choice will form
a single society. Thus, if the players choose unanimously, everyone will
live in the same society. The payoff structure of the game is superaddi-
tive (for all coalitions A and B, $v(A \cup B) > v(A) + v(B)$), owing to econo-
mies of scale, a lesser need for security measures, and so on. Thus,
everyone has a reason to select the same principles everyone else is
selecting, which provides the necessary degree of strategic interaction.
Since the game is completely symmetrical, if there is a unique rational
choice, everyone should make the same choice, and so the need for una-

29. Rawls, "A Brief Restatement," sec. 25, p. 70.

nimity will be met. Which principles of justice get chosen by the parties will determine which version of the second game they play.

In the second game, which I call the "society game," the parties, still behind the veil of ignorance, ask a different question. Having attempted to advance the interests of those they represent as best they could by choosing principles of justice, they now try to work out what will actually happen in a society that has been well ordered by the principles they have selected. This game is somewhat more difficult to conceive, as it has aspects that take place on both sides of the veil of ignorance. We might think of it as follows: The parties, still behind the veil, build, as best they can, a model of a real society, not behind the veil, in which the basic structure is governed by the principles they have chosen in the choice game. We can picture this by thinking of the parties setting up toy models of different societies and setting them running. In fact, this stage will be accomplished by deliberation about how the parties imagine a society guided by their chosen principles will turn out. Since they are given general facts about moral psychology and uncontroversial scientific knowledge, they will have the means necessary to make the sorts of arguments that Rawls himself makes when he argues for the stability of the two principles. Thus, the players in this second game are not the parties themselves, but people in a real society. Despite that, what we are really interested in is what the parties learn from watching this game played out. In particular, the parties behind the veil are concerned to find out whether a society not covered by the veil and guided by the principles they have chosen will be well ordered and stable in the right way. Another way of thinking about this game is that the parties are to apply Scanlon's question to imaginary members of the society they are designing, checking that there is no one who might reasonably reject the principles they chose in the first game. If it turns out that the choice made in the first game will be stable, then the constitutional convention game can begin with the chosen principles enshrined. If the choice turns out not to be stable, however, the parties must return to the choice game and try again. As we will see below, the society game plays the role of ensuring that the principles chosen in the choice game are in the least core of that game. In order for this to work, the parties will have to be able to move freely between the games, making tentative choices in the first game and checking them out in the second game, only to return to the first game if these choices turn out not to be stable.

Before discussing the nature of the stability required in each of these two games, let us examine more closely how the parties make their initial choice. In the choice game the players are, in essence, deciding which constitutional convention game they want to be played for their constituents' sake. Since they are unsure what will come out of various conventions, and this indeterminacy is further exacerbated by the full four-stage sequence of original position, constitutional convention, legislature, and judiciary, the parties have absolutely no way of determining even subjective probabilities about the final outcomes of those they represent in the fully realized society. They can, however, make general arguments about the nature of society, and what types of lives will be available given certain overriding principles of justice. Thus, they attempt to evaluate their options in terms of how each set of principles will affect their constituents in general terms. Equipped with the thin theory of the good, for instance, they know that having more primary goods is better than having fewer and that they will provide all-purpose means to pursue any reasonable comprehensive conception of the good. They also know that more utility is better than less. They can also make reasonable assumptions about the level of stability under different principles, and the stability game forces them to take these considerations explicitly into account. Clearly, however, they will not be able to assign precise values to different states of affairs, let alone different abstract principles of justice. Thus, in determining whether a given principle is in the core or the least core of the choice game, we will have to rely on the nature of the arguments that can be advanced in favor of it. In Section I we saw, both in the discussion of the least core and in the proof that the definition of fairness captured Scanlon's considerations, that arguments that something is in the core relied solely on an individual's or group's isolated claim in relation to how they could do on their own, while arguments placing principles or outcomes in the least core relied on the relationship between coalitions and strong notions of reciprocity. By drawing parallels between these sorts of arguments and those advanced by the parties for various parts of the two principles of justice, we can capture the spirit, if not the full mathematical precision, of the game-theoretic account of fairness.

As just stated, these remarks may seem more confusing than illuminating. In order to give them greater sense, let us examine the nature of the stability arising from each game, and then consider directly why the two principles are in the least core of the choice game that I have set out.

The first question of stability arises in connection with the initial choice of principles behind the veil of ignorance. Here, stability requires that the parties be content with their choice given the "strains of commitment"[30] their constituents are likely to have to endure. We continue to assume that the "special psychologies"[31] of envy, spite, and so on do not play a role. At this stage we are merely concerned that none of the people represented by the parties have grounds for wishing that their representatives had chosen differently. The type of complaint that would violate this stability condition might run as follows: "I wasn't guaranteed some liberty that I could have had with no (or acceptably few) sacrifices if my representative had made a different choice, and the lack of that liberty hampers my pursuit of the good as I conceive it."

Notice that complaints against this type of stability rely only on considerations of how a person actually did and what that person was guaranteed by the structure of the game. Thus, these are the kinds of complaints that arise because the chosen principles were not in the core of the choice game. As we will see below, in Rawls's latest formulation of the argument for the two principles of justice, these are the types of arguments that are used to settle on the first principle, the guarantee of equal basic liberties.

The second question of stability arises in connection with the society game, and requires focusing on society in general. We now allow the special psychologies free rein and see if they tear apart a society otherwise well ordered by the chosen principles. To determine this, we have to ask questions about whether society leads to the development of a "sense of justice"[32] and the development of a moral psychology under the chosen principles. The second question asks whether a society guided by a given set of principles would be in equilibrium in the more scientific meaning of the term, whether it would tend to correct problems brought about by irrationality, intolerance, envy, and so forth or whether these problems would tend to ferment and grow strong enough to make society unstable. Once again, these arguments are made by the

30. Rawls, *A Theory of Justice*, pp. 176ff.
31. Ibid., pp. 143ff. See also Rawls, "A Brief Restatement," sec. 25, pp. 71–72.
32. Rawls, *A Theory of Justice*, p. 567.

parties behind the veil of ignorance looking out into the real world (or what they suppose generally it will be like).

An example of the kind of complaint that will count against this type of stability is as follows: "I am poor, and she is rich, and because the principles that guide the distribution of income are publicly known, I know that her wealth in no way benefits me. I also know that there are alternative distributive principles under which I would be better off and, though she would be somewhat worse off, no one would be as badly off as I am now. As a result, I feel no degree of reciprocity with other members of society, especially those like her, and thus I have no interest in actively taking part in its institutions that benefit her at my expense." Notice that this argument relies both on considerations of how other people do under the principles in question and on the alternatives that are available. These complaints, then, are of the type that get made against outcomes in the core, but not the least core, of a game. They are also the kinds of reasons Rawls now gives for choosing the difference principle instead of a restricted form of average utilitarianism with a social minimum as the distributive principle to be added to the first principle.

We can now get a better sense of the role of the society game in the original position. If principles had only to be selected in the first game, then any principles in the core of that game would be equally likely candidates, since the types of arguments likely to be advanced in the deliberation about the initial choice of principles will be those for rejecting noncore outcomes only. In the society game, however, arguments will surface that will reject all but the principles in the least core of the choice game. Thus, the society game ensures that the principles that finally emerge from the original position are in the least core of the choice game, and thus that the fairness of the original position is preserved to as high a degree as possible at least into the constitutional convention.

A quick summary of the arguments Rawls now makes for why the parties in the original position choose the two principles of justice ought to make clear why they are in the least core of the original position games as I have laid them out. He divides up the argument into "two fundamental comparisons."[33] The first fundamental comparison argues for the two principles over a principle of average utility taken alone. This com-

---

33. Rawls, "A Brief Restatement," sec. 23, p. 65.

parison is meant to secure the first principle, and thus, claims Rawls, is the more important as well as the more decisive of the two.[34] To see why it secures the first principle, note that the arguments that follow would apply just as well to the first principle joined to any principle that provided for equality of opportunity and a reasonable distribution of wealth. The argument relies on the maximin rule for choice under uncertainty, and claims that there are three conditions, all of which obtain in the original position to a high degree, in the face of which it is rational to apply the maximin rule. These conditions are (1) that there is no way to assign probabilities to the outcomes, (2) that any improvements over the maximin level are relatively unimportant, and (3) that any shortfall below the maximin level would be disastrous. Rawls claims that these hold in the original position, and that since the basic liberties are guaranteed under the two principles and not under utilitarianism, it is the maximin and thus the rational choice to make.

Within the structure of the choice game I described, a further point can be made. Regardless of how the other players choose, it will be rational for each of the parties to select a set of principles that includes the guarantee of basic liberties for the reasons given above. Since the arguments advanced in the first fundamental comparison rely only on what each was guaranteed and eventually got, and no one playing the choice game would have a reason to change a strategy that selected the two principles over utilitarianism, the first fundamental comparison shows that the two principles are in the core of the choice game. Another way of thinking about this is that any set of principles of justice that includes the first principle will be in the core of the original position game and thus, at the very least, not unfair.

The second fundamental comparison is designed to argue for the difference principle. It compares the two principles of justice with a version of the two principles in which the difference principle is replaced with a principle of average utility with a social minimum. The argument here, Rawls claims, is less decisive, but relies on three types of interrelated reasons. These "fall under the ideas of publicity, reciprocity, and stability."[35] In outline, the argument runs as follows: Because the principles chosen in the original position will be publicly recognized as regulating

34. Ibid., sec. 27, p. 79.
35. Ibid., sec. 35, p. 99.

society, they will lead people to greater or lesser feelings of reciprocity
with others depending on to what extent they embody various degrees of
reciprocity. The greater the reciprocity that members of a society feel
with one another, the more likely they are to gain allegiance, over time,
to principles and institutions that embody that feeling, and thus the more
stable a society guided by those principles is likely to be. The difference
principle embodies a strong form of reciprocity to a very high degree, and
thus would be preferred to a principle of average utility with a social minimum that did not embody such a strong degree of reciprocity. Rawls
claims that the difference principle is the only distributive rule that
"meets the following reciprocity condition: those who are better off at
any point are not better off to the detriment of those who are worse off at
that point."[36]

Now, clearly, the type of argument invoked in the second comparison
turns on whether the two principles are in the least core of the choice
game. First of all, it requires a knowledge of how everyone is doing under
a certain principle and what alternatives are available. Second, the appeal to reciprocity is precisely the same as that made in my earlier arguments that outcomes in the core but not the least core of a game are
rejectable.

The result of the above argument shows that the two principles of justice are in the least core of the original position games that I have laid
out. But the difference principle, on one common reading of it, tells us
to always choose the outcome that maximizes the fortunes of the worst-
off, and thus can be read as telling us to pick the least core of the game
society ultimately plays. A question now arises: Why not just collapse
these successive invocations of the dictum "choose the least core"?

There are two answers, both of which should help clarify the point I
am trying to make. The first is that the difference principle is meant to
apply to systems of distribution and the principles that govern them, *not*
to the choice between specific allocations. Thus, the difference principle
is not, at least in the sense described above, a repeat of the direction
"choose the least core." The second answer is that there is a difference
between the derived fairness of metagames and the derived fairness of
standard games. As I already mentioned when discussing this distinction, one of the key differences is that in metagames, the choice of units

36. Ibid., sec. 36, p. 102.

is often still up for grabs. This is certainly true in the original position. Thus, part of what comes out of choosing a set of principles in the least core of the original position is that we decide that the proper index for distributive justice is primary goods (if we agree with Rawls, that is). At the level of the actual working of society, with the difference principle in effect, we evaluate different methods of distribution in terms of how many primary goods individuals can expect to receive over a full life. Here, the two principles of justice (as well as the proper constitution, laws, and judicial opinions) ensure the fairness of society by producing a distribution that is in the least core of a standard game whose outcomes are measured in primary goods. If we were to collapse these successive applications of least-core reasoning into one, we would need to specify units in advance. But then the argument would indeed be circular.

From a consideration of these two fundamental comparisons, it should now be clear how we can claim that principles are in the core or the least core of a game without attaching expected values to various probable final outcomes, while still invoking general considerations of the types of outcomes different principles will produce. We can also see more clearly how the society game, with its explicit concern for stability, ensures that the parties choose principles that are in the least core of the choice game, and the different degrees of fairness captured by each of the two principles of justice.

I want to end by making a structural point about Rawls's argument as a whole that also comes out of this game-theoretic reading, and that, I think, is one of the main advantages of such a reading. We just saw how the two-game approach allowed us to differentiate between types of stability. Returning to the theory of fairness, we can now connect them back together again. Recall that Rawls introduces the original position (specifically, what I called the choice problem) as a way to ensure that the principles of justice are fair. In terms of our game-theoretic definition of fairness, we can now see how the original position manages to do that. To begin with, Rawls starts from very strict assumptions about the information available to the parties in the original position. In this way he leaves no doubt that the parties behind the veil of ignorance are playing a fair game. In the terminology of the previous section, we might label the original position G_0.

A brief remark on the status of the original position might be helpful here. Remember that our definition of fairness required that the first

game in the series be a metagame. Thus, in order for the original position
to fit into our definition, it must be a metagame, and not merely a game
with standard payoffs.[37] This requirement is overlooked by almost every
author who attempts to discuss the choice made in the original position
in any formal fashion.[38] Standard models of the original position discuss
the allocation of goods, income, or utility from behind the veil of ignorance, and this approach has launched a great deal of criticism against
the difference principle for placing too much weight on the desires of the
least advantaged. The problem with such readings is that Rawls makes
it very clear throughout *A Theory of Justice* and in his recent writings
that the two principles of justice are to apply not to the allocation of resources but to the basic structure of society as a whole within which
distributions of goods come about—that they are principles of distributive rather than allocative justice.

If we treat the original position as a metagame, it is harder to miss this
point. For if the outcomes of the original position are other games, we
are less likely to collapse them into simple payoffs. The basic structure
of society, in turn, allows us to choose from several games that will be
played at more and more specific levels of society. In each case, however,
the fairness of the original position will be preserved as long as the
choices made are always within the least core of the game being played.

For the choice problem of the original position to assure the fairness
of the two principles of justice requires two things. The first is that the
original position be indisputably fair, which explains the importance of
the veil of ignorance, and the strict limit on information available to the
parties who are behind it. Thus, attempts to reduce the number of what
Binmore calls "fictions"[39] in an account of the initial contract situation
can only weaken the claims to fairness that the theory has as a whole.
Problems arise only when too much information is admitted into the original metagame. As the veil will be lifted during the four-stage sequence

37. Whether we choose to call the original position two metagames, one following from
the other, or a single metagame with two parts is entirely semantic. When talking about
the internal structure of the original position, it helps to refer to it as two games to emphasize the separateness of the two parts of the argument. When talking about the relation it
bears to the rest of the theory, it is convenient to refer to it as a single entity, as I do
throughout the rest of this section.

38. See, e.g., Harsanyi, "Can the Maximin Principle Serve?"; Howe and Roemer,
"Rawlsian Justice"; and Binmore, "Game Theory."

39. Binmore, "Social Contract I," p. 92.

in which the laws are progressively filled out to fit a particular society, any fictions will in due course be eliminated from the completed theory, and need not concern us in our formulation of the original position.

The second condition, which ensures that the fairness of the original position is preserved through the four-stage sequence and thus in the day-to-day dealing of society, is that at every phase in that sequence the next game chosen must be in the least core of the one being played. Thus, the two principles of justice need to be in the least core of the original position game, the constitution needs to be in the least core of the constitutional convention game, the laws need to be in the least core of the legislative game, and so on.[40]

Notice, however, that arguments for stability often settle on the fact that the two principles of justice are an equilibrium strategy for the representatives in the original position, and thus, over time, people in a society guided by the two principles are likely to gain allegiance to its institutions rather than lose it. Rawls, for instance, argues that the two principles of justice "are everyone's best reply, so to speak, to the corresponding demands of the others."[41] More important, perhaps, is the very fact that Rawls finds it necessary to argue at great length for the stability of the two principles. Regardless of whether we find his arguments for stability convincing—and the point I am making here does not require that they be successful—the fact is that they are integral to the success of the argument for the two principles from the original position. The considerations of stability are no mere addenda to the argument, but rather are intrinsic to the nature of the argument as a whole.

These two facts lead to what I think is the true strength of Rawls's conception of justice. Notice that any choice made in the original position must be in the least core if the original position is to have any purpose. But, the reasons Rawls gives for thinking that the two principles of justice will be stable in the right way are precisely the types of reasons that place the two principles in the least core of the original position

40. That the first of these relations holds has been argued for above. Rawls, however, never really discusses what happens in later stages of the sequence in any detail, and so we cannot go beyond the first stage here. In some sense, it will be necessary to show that the later games in Rawls's sequence also have nonempty cores before any defense of Rawls along these lines is absolutely complete. The enormity of Rawls's accomplishment in working out the first stage of the sequence excuses him from charges of incompleteness, and I hope the limited scope of this article gives me adequate defense against similar charges.

41. Rawls, *A Theory of Justice*, p. 119.

game. Thus, Rawls's insistence that the conception of justice chosen in the choice problem of the original position be stable in the society game (the parties are aware of the "strains of commitment"[42] when making their choice, and do not fully ratify their choice until checking in the society game that the chosen principles are stable)[43] guarantees that the fairness of the choice situation is preserved at least as far as the constitutional convention. Thus, there is a strong connection between the two parts of the original position argument. The fairness that goes into the first game is connected to the stability that emerges from the second through the concern in the first game for the strains of commitment that will arise in the second game. It should come as no surprise, then, that the argument in the second part upholds the principles chosen in the first.

My point here is not that Rawls has convincingly argued that the two principles of justice are stable, or even fair, although I think he has. Rather, the point is a structural one about the interworkings of the arguments, and can be accepted independently from the acceptance of Rawls's argument, although I think an acceptance of the structural point makes it easier to see Rawls's argument as compelling. The point is that there exists a link in justice as fairness between the question of stability and the question of fairness; a link which I believe to be the real foundation of the theory. In order to show that the principles of justice are stable, Rawls must make an argument about how the real world works, and why people will adhere to the principles after the veil has been lifted, why the two principles of justice engender stability of the second type. Gauthier sees this question, which he attributes to the Foole in Hobbes's *Leviathan*, as the main obstacle any contract theory must overcome. He states it in very clear terms: "What the Foole challenges is the third law [of Hobbes], the law requiring compliance, or adherence to one's covenants, for let it be ever so advantageous to make an agreement, may it not then be even more advantageous to violate the agreement made? And if advantageous, then is it not rational? The Foole challenges the heart of the connection between reason and morals that both Hobbes and we seek to establish—the rationality of accepting a moral constraint on the direct pursuit of one's greatest utility."[44]

42. Ibid., pp. 145, 176.
43. Ibid., pt. 3.
44. Gauthier, *Morals by Agreement*, p. 161.

What Rawls gains from his emphasis on fairness is that the link between choice and adherence becomes a necessary one. For if principles will not be adhered to, then they are not stable, and, more importantly from a game-theoretic perspective, they are not in the core.[45] But this alone is reason for not selecting them in the original position, for it means that they will not be fair, either. In Rawls's framework, a set of principles is either fair and stable or neither; thus his structure, if it stands up at all, works to strengthen itself.

45. Of course, it might be suggested that there is an even simpler reply open to Rawls (or at least my reading of him). Since the cooperative game theory used to set up the theory of fairness and model the original position relies on an ability to make binding agreements, it might be pointed out that questions of adherence are moot. I think, however, that Rawls has a stronger reply, one that will satisfy even noncooperative game theorists like Gauthier and Binmore. By making the stability of society an explicit concern of the parties in the original position, Rawls makes sure that there will be little or no strain placed on the commitments. Clearly, no hypothetical commitments can be made absolutely binding. The point is that people living in a society guided by the two principles of justice will have no reason to change the hypothetical agreement, and thus no wish to withdraw, recontract, or revolt. More can and should be said on this subject, but space limitations preclude its being said here.

ROSALIND HURSTHOUSE   Virtue Theory and Abortion

The sort of ethical theory derived from Aristotle, variously described as virtue ethics, virtue-based ethics, or neo-Aristotelianism, is becoming better known, and is now quite widely recognized as at least a possible rival to deontological and utilitarian theories. With recognition has come criticism, of varying quality. In this article I shall discuss nine separate criticisms that I have frequently encountered, most of which seem to me to betray an inadequate grasp either of the structure of virtue theory or of what would be involved in thinking about a real moral issue in its terms. In the first half I aim particularly to secure an understanding that will reveal that many of these criticisms are simply misplaced, and to articulate what I take to be the major criticism of virtue theory. I reject this criticism, but do not claim that it is necessarily misplaced. In the second half I aim to deepen that understanding and highlight the issues raised by the criticisms by illustrating what the theory looks like when it is applied to a particular issue, in this case, abortion.

Virtue Theory

Virtue theory can be laid out in a framework that reveals clearly some of the essential similarities and differences between it and some versions of deontological and utilitarian theories. I begin with a rough sketch of fa-

Versions of this article have been read to philosophy societies at University College, London, Rutgers University, and the Universities of Dundee, Edinburgh, Oxford, Swansea, and California–San Diego; at a conference of the Polish and British Academies in Cracow in 1988 on "Life, Death and the Law," and as a symposium paper at the Pacific Division of the American Philosophical Association in 1989. I am grateful to the many people who contributed to the discussions of it on these occasions, and particularly to Philippa Foot and Anne Jaap Jacobson for private discussion.

miliar versions of the latter two sorts of theory, not, of course, with the intention of suggesting that they exhaust the field, but on the assumption that their very familiarity will provide a helpful contrast with virtue theory. Suppose a deontological theory has basically the following framework. We begin with a premise providing a specification of right action:

P.1. An action is right iff it is in accordance with a moral rule or principle.

This is a purely formal specification, forging a link between the concepts of *right action* and *moral rule,* and gives one no guidance until one knows what a moral rule is. So the next thing the theory needs is a premise about that:

P.2. A moral rule is one that . . .

Historically, an acceptable completion of P.2 would have been

(i) is laid on us by God

or

(ii) is required by natural law.

In secular versions (not, of course, unconnected to God's being pure reason, and the universality of natural law) we get such completions as

(iii) is laid on us by reason

or

(iv) is required by rationality

or

(v) would command universal rational acceptance

or

(vi) would be the object of choice of all rational beings

and so on. Such a specification forges a second conceptual link, between the concepts of *moral rule* and *rationality.*

We have here the skeleton of a familiar version of a deontological theory, a skeleton that reveals that what is essential to any such version is the links between *right action, moral rule,* and *rationality.* That these form the basic structure can be seen particularly vividly if we lay out the familiar act-utilitarianism in such a way as to bring out the contrasts.

Act-utilitarianism begins with a premise that provides a specification of right action:

P.1. An action is right iff it promotes the best consequences.

It thereby forges the link between the concepts of *right action* and *consequences*. It goes on to specify what the best consequences are in its second premise:

P.2. The best consequences are those in which happiness is maximized.

It thereby forges the link between *consequences* and *happiness*.

Now let us consider what a skeletal virtue theory looks like. It begins with a specification of right action:

P.1. An action is right iff it is what a virtuous agent would do in the circumstances.[1]

This, like the first premises of the other two sorts of theory, is a purely formal principle, giving one no guidance as to what to do, that forges the conceptual link between *right action* and *virtuous agent*. Like the other theories, it must, of course, go on to specify what the latter is. The first step toward this may appear quite trivial, but is needed to correct a prevailing tendency among many critics to define the virtuous agent as one who is disposed to act in accordance with a deontologist's moral rules.

P.1a. A virtuous agent is one who acts virtuously, that is, one who has and exercises the virtues.

This subsidiary premise lays bare the fact that virtue theory aims to provide a nontrivial specification of the virtuous agent *via* a nontrivial specification of the virtues, which is given in its second premise:

1. It should be noted that this premise intentionally allows for the possibility that two virtuous agents, faced with the same choice in the same circumstances, may act differently. For example, one might opt for taking her father off the life-support machine and the other for leaving her father on it. The theory requires that neither agent thinks that what the other does is wrong (see note 4 below), but it explicitly allows that no action is uniquely right in such a case—both are right. It also intentionally allows for the possibility that in some circumstances—those into which no virtuous agent could have got herself— no action is right. I explore this premise at greater length in "Applying Virtue Ethics," forthcoming in a *festschrift* for Philippa Foot.

P.2. A virtue is a character trait a human being needs to flourish or live well.

This premise forges a conceptual link between *virtue* and *flourishing* (or *living well* or *eudaimonia*). And, just as deontology, in theory, then goes on to argue that each favored rule meets its specification, so virtue ethics, in theory, goes on to argue that each favored character trait meets its.

These are the bare bones of virtue theory. Following are five brief comments directed to some misconceived criticisms that should be cleared out of the way.

First, the theory does not have a peculiar weakness or problem in virtue of the fact that it involves the concept of *eudaimonia* (a standard criticism being that this concept is hopelessly obscure). Now no virtue theorist will pretend that the concept of human flourishing is an easy one to grasp. I will not even claim here (though I would elsewhere) that it is no more obscure than the concepts of *rationality* and *happiness*, since, if our vocabulary were more limited, we might, *faute de mieux*, call it (human) *rational happiness*, and thereby reveal that it has at least some of the difficulties of both. But virtue theory has never, so far as I know, been dismissed on the grounds of the *comparative* obscurity of this central concept; rather, the popular view is that it has a problem with this which deontology and utilitarianism in no way share. This, I think, is clearly false. Both *rationality* and *happiness*, as they figure in their respective theories, are rich and difficult concepts—hence all the disputes about the various tests for a rule's being an object of rational choice, and the disputes, dating back to Mill's introduction of the higher and lower pleasures, about what constitutes happiness.

Second, the theory is not trivially circular; it does not specify right action in terms of the virtuous agent and then immediately specify the virtuous agent in terms of right action. Rather, it specifies her in terms of the virtues, and then specifies these, not merely as dispositions to right action, but as the character traits (which are dispositions to feel and react as well as act in certain ways) required for *eudaimonia*.[2]

2. There is, of course, the further question of whether the theory eventually describes a larger circle and winds up relying on the concept of right action in its interpretation of *eudaimonia*. In denying that the theory is trivially circular, I do not pretend to answer this intricate question. It is certainly true that virtue theory does not claim that the correct conception of *eudaimonia* can be got from "an independent 'value-free' investigation of

Third, it does answer the question "What should I do?" as well as the question "What sort of person should I be?" (That is, it is not, as one of the catchphrases has it, concerned only with Being and not with Doing.)

Fourth, the theory does, to a certain extent, answer this question by coming up with rules or principles (contrary to the common claim that it does not come up with any rules or principles). Every virtue generates a positive instruction (act justly, kindly, courageously, honestly, etc.) and every vice a prohibition (do not act unjustly, cruelly, like a coward, dishonestly, etc.). So trying to decide what to do within the framework of virtue theory is not, as some people seem to imagine, necessarily a matter of taking one's favored candidate for a virtuous person and asking oneself, "What would they do in these circumstances?" (as if the raped fifteen-year-old girl might be supposed to say to herself, "Now would Socrates have an abortion if he were in my circumstances?" and as if someone who had never known or heard of anyone very virtuous were going to be left, according to the theory, with no way to decide what to do at all). The agent may instead ask herself, "If I were to do such and such now, would I be acting justly or unjustly (or neither), kindly or unkindly [and so on]?" I shall consider below the problem created by cases in which such a question apparently does not yield an answer to "What should I do?" (because, say, the alternatives are being unkind or being unjust); here my claim is only that it sometimes does—the agent may employ her concepts of the virtues and vices directly, rather than imagining what some hypothetical exemplar would do.

Fifth (a point that is implicit but should be made explicit), virtue theory is not committed to any sort of reductionism involving defining all of our moral concepts in terms of the virtuous agent. On the contrary, it relies on a lot of very significant moral concepts. Charity or benevolence, for instance, is the virtue whose concern is the *good* of others; that concept of *good* is related to the concept of *evil* or *harm*, and they are both related to the concepts of the *worthwhile*, the *advantageous*, and the *pleasant*. If I have the wrong conception of what is worthwhile and ad-

human nature" (John McDowell, "The Role of *Eudaimonia* in Aristotle's Ethics," in *Essays on Aristotle's Ethics*, ed. Amelie Rorty [Berkeley and Los Angeles: University of California Press, 1980]). The sort of training that is required for acquiring the correct conception no doubt involves being taught from early on such things as "Decent people do this sort of thing, not that" and "To do such and such is the mark of a depraved character" (cf. *Nicomachean Ethics* 1110a22). But whether this counts as relying on the concept of right (or wrong) action seems to me very unclear and requiring much discussion.

vantageous and pleasant, then I shall have the wrong conception of what is good for, and harmful to, myself and others, and, even with the best will in the world, will lack the virtue of charity, which involves getting all this right. (This point will be illustrated at some length in the second half of this article; I mention it here only in support of the fact that no virtue theorist who takes her inspiration from Aristotle would even contemplate aiming at reductionism.)[3]

Let me now, with equal brevity, run through two more standard criticisms of virtue theory (the sixth and seventh of my nine) to show that, though not entirely misplaced, they do not highlight problems peculiar to that theory but, rather, problems that are shared by familiar versions of deontology.

One common criticism is that we do not know which character traits are the virtues, or that this is open to much dispute, or particularly subject to the threat of moral skepticism or "pluralism"[4] or cultural relativism. But the parallel roles played by the second premises of both deontological and virtue theories reveal the way in which both sorts of theory share this problem. It is at the stage at which one tries to get the right conclusions to drop out of the bottom of one's theory that, *theoretically,* all the work has to be done. Rule deontologists know that they want to get "don't kill," "keep promises," "cherish your children," and so on as the rules that meet their specification, whatever it may be. They also know that any of these can be disputed, that some philosopher may claim, of any one of them, that it is reasonable to reject it, and that at least people claim that there has been, for each rule, some culture that

3. Cf. Bernard Williams' point in *Ethics and the Limits of Philosophy* (London: William Collins, 1985) that we need an enriched ethical vocabulary, not a cut-down one.

4. I put *pluralism* in scare quotes to serve as a warning that virtue theory is not incompatible with all forms of it. It allows for "competing conceptions" of *eudaimonia* and the worthwhile, for instance, in the sense that it allows for a plurality of flourishing lives—the theory need not follow Aristotle in specifying the life of contemplation as the only one that truly constitutes *eudaimonia* (if he does). But the conceptions "compete" only in the sense that, within a single flourishing life, not everything worthwhile can be fitted in; the theory does not allow that two people with a correct conception of *eudaimonia* can disagree over whether the way the other is living constitutes flourishing. Moreover, the theory is committed to the strong thesis that the same set of character traits is needed for *any* flourishing life; it will not allow that, for instance, soldiers need courage but wives and mothers do not, or that judges need justice but can live well despite lacking kindness. (This obviously is related to the point made in note 1 above.) For an interesting discussion of pluralism (different interpretations thereof) and virtue theory, see Douglas B. Rasmussen, "Liberalism and Natural End Ethics," *American Philosophical Quarterly* 27 (1990): 153–61.

rejected it. Similarly, the virtue theorists know that they want to get jus-tice, charity, fidelity, courage, and so on as the character traits needed for *eudaimonia*; and they also know that any of these can be disputed, that some philosopher will say of any one of them that it is reasonable to reject it as a virtue, and that there is said to be, for each character trait, some culture that has thus rejected it.

This is a problem for both theories, and the virtue theorist certainly does not find it any harder to argue against moral skepticism, "plural-ism," or cultural relativism than the deontologist. Each theory has to stick out its neck and say, in some cases, "This person/these people/other cultures are (or would be) in error," and find some grounds for saying this.

Another criticism (the seventh) often made is that virtue ethics has unresolvable conflict built into it. "It is common knowledge," it is said, "that the requirements of the virtues can conflict; charity may prompt me to end the frightful suffering of the person in my care by killing him, but justice bids me to stay my hand. To tell my brother that his wife is being unfaithful to him would be honest and loyal, but it would be kinder to keep quiet about it. So which should I do? In such cases, virtue ethics has nothing helpful to say." (This is one version of the problem, men-tioned above, that considering whether a proposed action falls under a virtue or vice term does not always yield an answer to "What should I do?")

The obvious reply to this criticism is that rule deontology notoriously suffers from the same problem, arising not only from the fact that its rules can apparently conflict, but also from the fact that, at first blush, it appears that one and the same rule (e.g., preserve life) can yield contrary instructions in a particular case.[5] As before, I agree that this is a problem for virtue theory, but deny that it is a problem peculiar to it.

Finally, I want to articulate, and reject, what I take to be the major criticism of virtue theory. Perhaps because it is *the* major criticism, the reflection of a very general sort of disquiet about the theory, it is hard to state clearly—especially for someone who does not accept it—but it goes something like this.[6] My interlocutor says:

5. E.g., in Williams' Jim and Pedro case in J.J.C. Smart and Bernard Williams, *Utilitar-ianism: For and Against* (London: Cambridge University Press, 1973).

6. Intimations of this criticism constantly come up in discussion; the clearest statement of it I have found is by Onora O'Neill, in her review of Stephen Clark's *The Moral Status*

Virtue theory can't *get* us anywhere in real moral issues because it's bound to be all assertion and no argument. You admit that the best it can come up with in the way of action-guiding rules are the ones that rely on the virtue and vice concepts, such as "act charitably," "don't act cruelly," and so on; and, as if that weren't bad enough, you admit that these virtue concepts, such as charity, presuppose concepts such as the *good*, and the *worthwhile*, and so on. But that means that any virtue theorist who writes about real moral issues must rely on her audience's agreeing with her application of all these concepts, and hence accepting all the premises in which those applications are enshrined. But some other virtue theorist might take different premises about these matters, and come up with very different conclusions, and, within the terms of the theory, there is no way to distinguish between the two. While there is agreement, virtue theory can repeat conventional wisdom, preserve the status quo, but it can't get us anywhere in the way that a normative ethical theory is supposed to, namely, by providing rational grounds for acceptance of its practical conclusions.

My strategy will be to split this criticism into two: one (the eighth) addressed to the virtue theorist's employment of the virtue and vice concepts enshrined in her rules—act charitably, honestly, and so on—and the other (the ninth) addressed to her employment of concepts such as that of the *worthwhile*. Each objection, I shall maintain, implicitly appeals to a certain *condition of adequacy* on a normative moral theory, and in each case, I shall claim, the condition of adequacy, once made explicit, is utterly implausible.

It is true that when she discusses real moral issues, the virtue theorist has to assert that certain actions are honest, dishonest, or neither; charitable, uncharitable, or neither. And it is true that this is often a very difficult matter to decide; her rules are not always easy to apply. But this counts as a criticism of the theory only if we assume, as a condition of adequacy, that any adequate action-guiding theory must make the difficult business of knowing what to do if one is to act well easy, that it must provide clear guidance about what ought and ought not to be done which

---

of Animals, in *Journal of Philosophy* 77 (1980): 440–46. For a response I am much in sympathy with, see Cora Diamond, "Anything But Argument?" *Philosophical Investigations* 5 (1982): 23–41.

any reasonably clever adolescent could follow if she chose. But such a condition of adequacy is implausible. Acting rightly *is* difficult, and *does* call for much moral wisdom, and the relevant condition of adequacy, which virtue theory meets, is that it should have built into it an explanation of a truth expressed by Aristotle,[7] namely, that moral knowledge—unlike mathematical knowledge—cannot be acquired merely by attending lectures and is not characteristically to be found in people too young to have had much experience of life. There are youthful mathematical geniuses, but rarely, if ever, youthful moral geniuses, and this tells us something significant about the sort of knowledge that moral knowledge is. Virtue ethics builds this in straight off precisely by couching its rules in terms whose application may indeed call for the most delicate and sensitive judgment.

Here we may discern a slightly different version of the problem that there are cases in which applying the virtue and vice terms does not yield an answer to "What should I do?" Suppose someone "youthful in character," as Aristotle puts it, having applied the relevant terms, finds herself landed with what is, unbeknownst to her, a case not of real but of apparent conflict, arising from a misapplication of those terms. Then she will not be able to decide what to do unless she knows of a virtuous agent to look to for guidance. But her quandary is (*ex hypothesi*) the result of her lack of wisdom, and just what virtue theory expects. Someone hesitating over whether to reveal a hurtful truth, for example, thinking it would be kind but dishonest or unjust to lie, may need to realize, with respect to these particular circumstances, not that kindness is more (or less) important than honesty or justice, and not that honesty or justice sometimes requires one to act unkindly or cruelly, but that one does people no kindness by concealing this sort of truth from them, hurtful as it may be. This is the *type* of thing (I use it only as an example) that people with moral wisdom know about, involving the correct application of *kind*, and that people without such wisdom find difficult.

What about the virtue theorist's reliance on concepts such as that of the *worthwhile*? If such reliance is to count as a fault in the theory, what condition of adequacy is implicitly in play? It must be that any good normative theory should provide answers to questions about real moral issues whose truth is in no way determined by truths about what is worth-

7. Aristotle, *Nicomachean Ethics* 1142a12–16.

while, or what really matters in human life. Now although people are initially inclined to reject out of hand the claim that the practical conclusions of a normative moral theory have to be based on premises about what is truly worthwhile, the alternative, once it is made explicit, may look even more unacceptable. Consider what the condition of adequacy entails. If truths about what is worthwhile (or truly good, or serious, or about what matters in human life) do *not* have to be appealed to in order to answer questions about real moral issues, then I might sensibly seek guidance about what I ought to do from someone who had declared in advance that she knew nothing about such matters, or from someone who said that, although she had opinions about them, these were quite likely to be wrong but that this did not matter, because they would play no determining role in the advice she gave me.

I should emphasize that we are talking about real moral issues and real guidance; I want to know whether I should have an abortion, take my mother off the life-support machine, leave academic life and become a doctor in the Third World, give up my job with the firm that is using animals in its experiments, tell my father he has cancer. Would I go to someone who says she has *no* views about what is worthwhile in life? Or to someone who says that, as a matter of fact, she tends to think that the only thing that matters is having a good time, but has a normative theory that is consistent both with this view and with my own rather more puritanical one, which will yield the guidance I need?

I take it as a premise that this is absurd. The relevant condition of adequacy should be that the practical conclusions of a good normative theory *must* be in part determined by premises about what is worthwhile, important, and so on. Thus I reject this "major criticism" of virtue theory, that it cannot get us anywhere in the way that a normative moral theory is supposed to. According to my response, a normative theory that any clever adolescent can apply, or that reaches practical conclusions that are in no way determined by premises about what is truly worthwhile, serious, and so on, is guaranteed to be an inadequate theory.

Although I reject this criticism, I have not argued that it is misplaced and that it necessarily manifests a failure to understand what virtue theory is. My rejection is based on premises about what an adequate normative theory must be like—what sorts of concepts it must contain, and what sort of account it must give of moral knowledge—and thereby claims, implicitly, that the "major criticism" manifests a failure to understand what an *adequate normative theory* is. But, as a matter of fact, I think the criticism is often made by people who have no idea of what virtue theory looks like when applied to a real moral issue; they drastically underestimate the variety of ways in which the virtue and vice concepts, and the others, such as that of the *worthwhile*, figure in such discussion.

As promised, I now turn to an illustration of such discussion, applying virtue theory to abortion. Before I embark on this tendentious business, I should remind the reader of the aim of this discussion. I am not, in this article, trying to solve the problem of abortion; I am illustrating how virtue theory directs one to think about it. It might indeed be said that thinking about the problem in this way "solves" it by *dis*solving it, insofar as it leads one to the conclusion that there is no single right answer, but a variety of particular answers, and in what follows I am certainly trying to make that conclusion seem plausible. But, that granted, it should still be said that I am not trying to "solve the problems" in the practical sense of telling people that they should, or should not, do this or that if they are pregnant and contemplating abortion in these or those particular circumstances.

I do not assume, or expect, that all of my readers will agree with everything I am about to say. On the contrary, given the plausible assumption that some are morally wiser than I am, and some less so, the theory has built into it that we are bound to disagree on some points. For instance, we may well disagree about the particular application of some of the virtue and vice terms; and we may disagree about what is worthwhile or serious, worthless or trivial. But my aim is to make clear how these concepts figure in a discussion conducted in terms of virtue theory. What is at issue is whether these concepts are indeed the ones that should come in, that is, whether virtue theory should be criticized for employing them. The problem of abortion highlights this issue dramatically since virtue theory quite transforms the discussion of it.

ABORTION

As everyone knows, the morality of abortion is commonly discussed in relation to just two considerations: first, and predominantly, the status of the fetus and whether or not it is the sort of thing that may or may not be innocuously or justifiably killed; and second, and less predominantly (when, that is, the discussion concerns the *morality* of abortion rather than the question of permissible legislation in a just society), women's rights. If one thinks within this familiar framework, one may well be puzzled about what virtue theory, as such, could contribute. Some people assume the discussion will be conducted solely in terms of what the virtuous agent would or would not do (cf. the third, fourth, and fifth criticisms above). Others assume that only justice, or at most justice and charity,[8] will be applied to the issue, generating a discussion very similar to Judith Jarvis Thomson's.[9]

Now if this is the way the virtue theorist's discussion of abortion is imagined to be, no wonder people think little of it. It seems obvious in advance that in any such discussion there must be either a great deal of extremely tendentious application of the virtue terms *just, charitable*, and so on or a lot of rhetorical appeal to "this is what only the virtuous agent knows." But these are caricatures; they fail to appreciate the way in which virtue theory quite transforms the discussion of abortion by dismissing the two familiar dominating considerations as, in a way, fundamentally irrelevant. In what way or ways, I hope to make both clear and plausible.

Let us first consider women's rights. Let me emphasize again that we are discussing the *morality* of abortion, not the rights and wrongs of laws prohibiting or permitting it. If we suppose that women do have a moral right to do as they choose with their own bodies, or, more particularly, to terminate their pregnancies, then it may well follow that a *law* forbidding abortion would be unjust. Indeed, even if they have no such right, such a law might be, as things stand at the moment, unjust, or impractical, or inhumane: on this issue I have nothing to say in this article. But, putting all questions about the justice or injustice of laws to one side, and sup-

---

8. It seems likely that some people have been misled by Foot's discussion of euthanasia (through no fault of hers) into thinking that a virtue theorist's discussion of terminating human life will be conducted exclusively in terms of justice and charity (and the corresponding vice terms) (Philippa Foot, "Euthanasia," *Philosophy & Public Affairs* 6, no. 2 [Winter 1977]: 85–112). But the act-category *euthanasia* is a very special one, at least as defined in her article, since such an act must be done "for the sake of the one who is to die." Building a virtuous motivation into the specification of the act in this way immediately rules out the application of many other vice terms.

9. Judith Jarvis Thomson, "A Defense of Abortion," *Philosophy & Public Affairs* 1, no. 1 (Fall 1971): 47–66. One could indeed regard this article as proto–virtue theory (no doubt to the surprise of the author) if the concepts of callousness and kindness were allowed more weight.

posing only that women have such a moral right, *nothing* follows from this supposition about the morality of abortion, according to virtue theory, once it is noted (quite generally, not with particular reference to abortion) that in exercising a moral right I can do something cruel, or callous, or selfish, light-minded, self-righteous, stupid, inconsiderate, disloyal, dishonest—that is, act viciously.[10] Love and friendship do not survive their parties' constantly insisting on their rights, nor do people live well when they think that getting what they have a right to is of preeminent importance; they harm others, and they harm themselves. So whether women have a moral right to terminate their pregnancies is irrelevant within virtue theory, for it is irrelevant to the question "In having an abortion in these circumstances, would the agent be acting virtuously or viciously or neither?"

What about the consideration of the status of the fetus—what can virtue theory say about that? One might say that this issue is not in the province of *any* moral theory; it is a metaphysical question, and an extremely difficult one at that. Must virtue theory then wait upon metaphysics to come up with the answer?

At first sight it might seem so. For virtue is said to involve knowledge, and part of this knowledge consists in having the *right* attitude to things. "Right" here does not just mean "morally right" or "proper" or "nice" in the modern sense; it means "accurate, true." One cannot have the right or correct attitude to something if the attitude is based on or involves false beliefs. And this suggests that if the status of the fetus is relevant to the rightness or wrongness of abortion, its status must be known, as a truth, to the fully wise and virtuous person.

But the sort of wisdom that the fully virtuous person has is not supposed to be recondite; it does not call for fancy philosophical sophistication, and it does not depend upon, let alone wait upon, the discoveries of academic philosophers.[11] And this entails the following, rather startling,

---

10. One possible qualification: if one ties the concept of justice very closely to rights, then if women do have a moral right to terminate their pregnancies it *may* follow that in doing so they do not act unjustly. (Cf. Thomson, "A Defense of Abortion.") But it is debatable whether even that much follows.

11. This is an assumption of virtue theory, and I do not attempt to defend it here. An adequate discussion of it would require a separate article, since, although most moral philosophers would be chary of claiming that intellectual sophistication is a necessary condition of moral wisdom or virtue, most of us, from Plato onward, tend to write as if this were so. Sorting out which claims about moral knowledge are committed to this kind of elitism

conclusion: that the status of the fetus—that issue over which so much ink has been spilt—is, according to virtue theory, simply not relevant to the rightness or wrongness of abortion (within, that is, a secular morality).

Or rather, since that is clearly too radical a conclusion, it is in a sense relevant, but only in the sense that the familiar biological facts are relevant. By "the familiar biological facts" I mean the facts that most human societies are and have been familiar with—that, standardly (but not invariably), pregnancy occurs as the result of sexual intercourse, that it lasts about nine months, during which time the fetus grows and develops, that standardly it terminates in the birth of a living baby, and that this is how we all come to be.

It might be thought that this distinction—between the familiar biological facts and the status of the fetus—is a distinction without a difference. But this is not so. To attach relevance to the status of the fetus, in the sense in which virtue theory claims it is not relevant, is to be gripped by the conviction that we must go beyond the familiar biological facts, deriving some sort of conclusion from them, such as that the fetus has rights, or is not a person, or something similar. It is also to believe that this exhausts the relevance of the familiar biological facts, that all they are relevant to is the status of the fetus and whether or not it is the sort of thing that may or may not be killed.

These convictions, I suspect, are rooted in the desire to solve the problem of abortion by getting it to fall under some general rule such as "You ought not to kill anything with the right to life but may kill anything else." But they have resulted in what should surely strike any nonphilosopher as a most bizarre aspect of nearly all the current philosophical literature on abortion, namely, that, far from treating abortion as a unique moral problem, markedly unlike any other, nearly everything written on the status of the fetus and its bearing on the abortion issue would be consistent with the human reproductive facts' (to say nothing of family life) being totally different from what they are. Imagine that you are an alien extraterrestrial anthropologist who does not know that the human race is roughly 50 percent female and 50 percent male, or that our only (natural) form of reproduction involves heterosexual intercourse, vivipa-

---

and which can, albeit with difficulty, be reconciled with the idea that moral knowledge can be acquired by anyone who really wants it would be a major task.

rous birth, and the female's (and only the female's) being pregnant for nine months, or that females are capable of childbearing from late childhood to late middle age, or that childbearing is painful, dangerous, and emotionally charged—do you think you would pick up these facts from the hundreds of articles written on the status of the fetus? I am quite sure you would not. And that, I think, shows that the current philosophical literature on abortion has got badly out of touch with reality.

Now if we are using virtue theory, our first question is not "What do the familiar biological facts show—what can be derived from them about the status of the fetus?" but "How do these facts figure in the practical reasoning, actions and passions, thoughts and reactions, of the virtuous and the nonvirtuous? What is the mark of having the right attitude to these facts and what manifests having the wrong attitude to them?" This immediately makes essentially relevant not only all the facts about human reproduction I mentioned above, but a whole range of facts about our emotions in relation to them as well. I mean such facts as that human parents, both male and female, tend to care passionately about their offspring, and that family relationships are among the deepest and strongest in our lives—and, significantly, among the longest-lasting.

These facts make it obvious that pregnancy is not just one among many other physical conditions; and hence that anyone who genuinely believes that an abortion is comparable to a haircut or an appendectomy is mistaken.[12] The fact that the premature termination of a pregnancy is, in some sense, the cutting off of a new human life, and thereby, like the procreation of a new human life, connects with all our thoughts about human life and death, parenthood, and family relationships, must make it a serious matter. To disregard this fact about it, to think of abortion as

12. Mary Anne Warren, in "On the Moral and Legal Status of Abortion," *Monist* 57 (1973), sec. 1, says of the opponents of restrictive laws governing abortion that "their conviction (for the most part) is that abortion is not a *morally* serious and extremely unfortunate, even though sometimes justified, act, comparable to killing in self-defense or to letting the violinist die, but rather is closer to being a *morally neutral* act, like cutting one's hair" (italics mine). I would like to think that no one *genuinely* believes this. But certainly in discussion, particularly when arguing against restrictive laws or the suggestion that remorse over abortion might be appropriate, I have found that some people *say* they believe it (and often cite Warren's article, albeit inaccurately, despite its age). Those who allow that it is morally serious, and far from morally neutral, have to argue against restrictive laws, or the appropriateness of remorse, on a very different ground from that laid down by the premise "The fetus is just part of the woman's body (and she has a right to determine what happens to her body and should not feel guilt about anything she does to it)."

nothing but the killing of something that does not matter, or as nothing but the exercise of some right or rights one has, or as the incidental means to some desirable state of affairs, is to do something callous and light-minded, the sort of thing that no virtuous and wise person would do. It is to have the wrong attitude not only to fetuses, but more generally to human life and death, parenthood, and family relationships.

Although I say that the facts make this obvious, I know that this is one of my tendentious points. In partial support of it I note that even the most dedicated proponents of the view that deliberate abortion is just like an appendectomy or haircut rarely hold the same view of spontaneous abortion, that is, miscarriage. It is not so tendentious of me to claim that to react to people's grief over miscarriage by saying, or even thinking, "What a fuss about nothing!" would be callous and light-minded, whereas to try to laugh someone out of grief over an appendectomy scar or a botched haircut would not be. It is hard to give this point due prominence within act-centered theories, for the inconsistency is an inconsistency in attitude about the seriousness of loss of life, not in beliefs about which acts are right or wrong. Moreover, an act-centered theorist may say, "Well, there is nothing wrong with *thinking* 'What a fuss about nothing!' as long as you do not say it and hurt the person who is grieving. And besides, we cannot be held responsible for our thoughts, only for the intentional actions they give rise to." But the character traits that virtue theory emphasizes are not simply dispositions to intentional actions, but a seamless disposition to certain actions and passions, thoughts and reactions.

To say that the cutting off of a human life is always a matter of some seriousness, at any stage, is not to deny the relevance of gradual fetal development. Notwithstanding the well-worn point that clear boundary lines cannot be drawn, our emotions and attitudes regarding the fetus do change as it develops, and again when it is born, and indeed further as the baby grows. Abortion for shallow reasons in the later stages is much more shocking than abortion for the same reasons in the early stages in a way that matches the fact that deep grief over miscarriage in the later stages is more appropriate than it is over miscarriage in the earlier stages (when, that is, the grief is solely about the loss of *this* child, not about, as might be the case, the loss of one's only hope of having a child or of having one's husband's child). Imagine (or recall) a woman who already has children; she had not intended to have more, but finds herself unexpectedly pregnant. Though contrary to her plans, the pregnancy, once established as a fact, is welcomed—and then she loses the embryo almost immediately. If this were bemoaned as a tragedy, it would, I think, be a misapplication of the concept of what is tragic. But it may still properly be mourned as a loss. The grief is expressed in such terms as "I shall always wonder how she or he would have turned out" or "When I look at the others, I shall think, 'How different their lives would have been if this other one had been part of them.' " It would, I take it, be callous and light-minded to say, or think, "Well, she has already *got* four children; what's the problem?"; it would be neither, nor arrogantly intrusive in the case of a close friend, to try to correct prolonged mourning by saying, "I know it's sad, but it's not a tragedy; rejoice in the ones you have." The application of *tragic* becomes more appropriate as the fetus grows, for the mere fact that one has lived with it for longer, conscious of its existence, makes a difference. To shrug off an early abortion is understandable just because it is very hard to be fully conscious of the fetus's existence in the early stages and hence hard to appreciate that an early abortion is the destruction of life. It is particularly hard for the young and inexperienced to appreciate this, because appreciation of it usually comes only with experience.

  I do not mean "with the experience of having an abortion" (though that may be part of it) but, quite generally, "with the experience of life." Many women who have borne children contrast their later pregnancies with their first successful one, saying that in the later ones they were conscious of a new life growing in them from very early on. And, more generally, as one reaches the age at which the next generation is coming up close behind one, the counterfactuals "If I, or she, had had an abortion, Alice, or Bob, would not have been born" acquire a significant application, which casts a new light on the conditionals "If I or Alice have an abortion then some Caroline or Bill will not be born."

The fact that pregnancy is not just one among many physical conditions does not mean that one can never regard it in that light without manifesting a vice. When women are in very poor physical health, or worn out from childbearing, or forced to do very physically demanding jobs, then they cannot be described as self-indulgent, callous, irresponsible, or light-minded if they seek abortions mainly with a view to avoiding pregnancy as the physical condition that it is. To go through with a pregnancy when one is utterly exhausted, or when one's job consists of crawling along tunnels hauling coal, as many women in the nineteenth century were obliged to do, is perhaps heroic, but people who do not achieve heroism are not necessarily vicious. That they can view the pregnancy only as eight months of misery, followed by hours if not days of agony and exhaustion, and abortion only as the blessed escape from this prospect, is entirely understandable and does not manifest any lack of serious respect for human life or a shallow attitude to motherhood. What it does show is that something is terribly amiss in the conditions of their lives, which make it so hard to recognize pregnancy and childbearing as the good that they can be.

In relation to this last point I should draw attention to the way in which virtue theory has a sort of built-in indexicality. Philosophers arguing against anything remotely resembling a belief in the sanctity of life (which the above claims clearly embody) frequently appeal to the existence of other communities in which abortion and infanticide are practiced. We should not automatically assume that it is impossible that some other communities could be morally inferior to our own; maybe some are, or have been, precisely insofar as their members are, typically, callous or light-minded or unjust. But in communities in which life is a great deal tougher for everyone than it is in ours, having the right attitude to human life and death, parenthood, and family relationships might well manifest itself in ways that are unlike ours. When it is essential to survival that most members of the community fend for themselves at a very young age or work during most of their waking hours, selective abortion or infanticide might be practiced either as a form of genuine euthanasia or for the sake of the community and not, I think, be thought callous or light-minded. But this does not make everything all right; as before, it shows that there is something amiss with the conditions of their lives, which are making it impossible for them to live really well.[13]

The foregoing discussion, insofar as it emphasizes the right attitude to human life and death, parallels to a certain extent those standard discussions of abortion that concentrate on it solely as an issue of killing. But it does not, as those discussions do, gloss over the fact, emphasized by those who discuss the morality of abortion in terms of women's rights, that abortion, wildly unlike any other form of killing, is the termination

13. For another example of the way in which "tough conditions" can make a difference to what is involved in having the right attitude to human life and death and family relationships, see the concluding sentences of Foot's "Euthanasia."

of a pregnancy, which is a condition of a woman's body and results in *her* having a child if it is not aborted. This fact is given due recognition not by appeal to women's rights but by emphasizing the relevance of the familiar biological and psychological facts and their connection with having the right attitude to parenthood and family relationships. But it may well be thought that failing to bring in women's rights still leaves some important aspects of the problem of abortion untouched.

Speaking in terms of women's rights, people sometimes say things like, "Well, it's her life you're talking about too, you know; she's got a right to her own life, her own happiness." And the discussion stops there. But in the context of virtue theory, given that we are particularly concerned with what constitutes a good human life, with what true happiness or *eudaimonia* is, this is no place to stop. We go on to ask, "And is this life of hers a good one? Is she living well?"

If we are to go on to talk about good human lives, in the context of abortion, we have to bring in our thoughts about the value of love and family life, and our proper emotional development through a natural life cycle. The familiar facts support the view that parenthood in general, and motherhood and childbearing in particular, are intrinsically worthwhile, are among the things that can be correctly thought to be partially constitutive of a flourishing human life.[14] If this is right, then a woman who opts for not being a mother (at all, or again, or now) by opting for abortion may thereby be manifesting a flawed grasp of what her life should be, and be about—a grasp that is childish, or grossly materialistic, or shortsighted, or shallow.

I said "*may* thereby": this *need* not be so. Consider, for instance, a woman who has already had several children and fears that to have another will seriously affect her capacity to be a good mother to the ones she has—she does not show a lack of appreciation of the intrinsic value of being a parent by opting for abortion. Nor does a woman who has been a good mother and is approaching the age at which she may be looking forward to being a good grandmother. Nor does a woman who discovers that her pregnancy may well kill her, and opts for abortion and adoption. Nor, necessarily, does a woman who has decided to lead a life centered

14. I take this as a premise here, but argue for it in some detail in my *Beginning Lives* (Oxford: Basil Blackwell, 1987). In this connection I also discuss adoption and the sense in which it may be regarded as "second best," and the difficult question of whether the good of parenthood may properly be sought, or indeed bought, by surrogacy.

around some other worthwhile activity or activities with which motherhood would compete.

People who are childless by choice are sometimes described as "irresponsible," or "selfish," or "refusing to grow up," or "not knowing what
life is about." But one can hold that having children is intrinsically
worthwhile without endorsing this, for we are, after all, in the happy position of there being more worthwhile things to do than can be fitted into
one lifetime. Parenthood, and motherhood in particular, even if granted
to be intrinsically worthwhile, undoubtedly take up a lot of one's adult
life, leaving no room for some other worthwhile pursuits. But some
women who choose abortion rather than have their first child, and some
men who encourage their partners to choose abortion, are not avoiding
parenthood for the sake of other worthwhile pursuits, but for the worthless one of "having a good time," or for the pursuit of some false vision
of the ideals of freedom or self-realization. And some others who say "I
am not ready for parenthood yet" are making some sort of mistake about
the extent to which one can manipulate the circumstances of one's life
so as to make it fulfill some dream that one has. Perhaps one's dream is
to have two perfect children, a girl and a boy, within a perfect marriage,
in financially secure circumstances, with an interesting job of one's own.
But to care too much about that dream, to demand of life that it give it
to one and act accordingly, may be both greedy and foolish, and is to run
the risk of missing out on happiness entirely. Not only may fate make
the dream impossible, or destroy it, but one's own attachment to it may
make it impossible. Good marriages, and the most promising children,
can be destroyed by just one adult's excessive demand for perfection.

Once again, this is not to deny that girls may quite properly say "I am
not ready for motherhood yet," especially in our society, and, far from
manifesting irresponsibility or light-mindedness, show an appropriate
modesty or humility, or a fearfulness that does not amount to cowardice.
However, even when the decision to have an abortion is the right decision—one that does not itself fall under a vice-related term and thereby
one that the perfectly virtuous could recommend—it does not follow that
there is no sense in which having the abortion is wrong, or guilt inappro-
priate. For, by virtue of the fact that a human life has been cut short,
some evil has probably been brought about,[15] and that circumstances

15. I say "some evil has probably been brought about" on the ground that (human) life

make the decision to bring about some evil the right decision will be a ground for guilt if getting into those circumstances in the first place itself manifested a flaw in character.

What "gets one into those circumstances" in the case of abortion is, except in the case of rape, one's sexual activity and one's choices, or the lack of them, about one's sexual partner and about contraception. The virtuous woman (which here of course does not mean simply "chaste woman" but "woman with the virtues") has such character traits as strength, independence, resoluteness, decisiveness, self-confidence, responsibility, serious-mindedness, and self-determination—and no one, I think, could deny that many women become pregnant in circumstances in which they cannot welcome or cannot face the thought of having *this* child precisely because they lack one or some of these character traits. So even in the cases where the decision to have an abortion is the right one, it can still be the reflection of a moral failing—not because the decision itself is weak or cowardly or irresolute or irresponsible or light-minded, but because lack of the requisite opposite of these failings landed one in the circumstances in the first place. Hence the common universalized claim that guilt and remorse are never appropriate emotions about an abortion is denied. They may be appropriate, and appropriately inculcated, even when the decision was the right one.

Another motivation for bringing women's rights into the discussion may be to attempt to correct the implication, carried by the killing-centered approach, that insofar as abortion is wrong, it is a wrong that only women do, or at least (given the preponderance of male doctors) that only women instigate. I do not myself believe that we can thus escape the fact that nature bears harder on women than it does on men,[16] but virtue theory can certainly correct many of the injustices that the emphasis on women's rights is rightly concerned about. With very little amendment, everything that has been said above applies to boys and men too. Although the abortion decision is, in a natural sense, the woman's decision, proper to her, boys and men are often party to it, for well

---

is (usually) a good and hence (human) death usually an evil. The exceptions would be (*a*) where death is actually a good or a benefit, because the baby that would come to be if the life were not cut short would be better off dead than alive, and (*b*) where death, though not a good, is not an evil either, because the life that would be led (e.g., in a state of permanent coma) would not be a good. (See Foot, "Euthanasia.")

16. I discuss this point at greater length in *Beginning Lives*.

or ill, and even when they are not, they are bound to have been party to the circumstances that brought it up. No less than girls and women, boys and men can, in their actions, manifest self-centeredness, callousness, and light-mindedness about life and parenthood in relation to abortion. They can be self-centered or courageous about the possibility of disability in their offspring; they need to reflect on their sexual activity and their choices, or the lack of them, about their sexual partner and contraception; they need to grow up and take responsibility for their own actions and life in relation to fatherhood. If it is true, as I maintain, that insofar as motherhood is intrinsically worthwhile, being a mother is an important purpose in women's lives, being a father (rather than a mere generator) is an important purpose in men's lives as well, and it is adolescent of men to turn a blind eye to this and pretend that they have many more important things to do.

CONCLUSION

Much more might be said, but I shall end the actual discussion of the problem of abortion here, and conclude by highlighting what I take to be its significant features. These hark back to many of the criticisms of virtue theory discussed earlier.

The discussion does not proceed simply by our trying to answer the question "Would a perfectly virtuous agent ever have an abortion and, if so, when?"; virtue theory is not limited to considering "Would Socrates have had an abortion if he were a raped, pregnant fifteen-year-old?" nor automatically stumped when we are considering circumstances into which no virtuous agent would have got herself. Instead, much of the discussion proceeds in the virtue- and vice-related terms whose application, in several cases, yields practical conclusions (cf. the third and fourth criticisms above). These terms are difficult to apply correctly, and anyone might challenge my application of any one of them. So, for example, I have claimed that some abortions, done for certain reasons, would be callous or light-minded; that others might indicate an appropriate modesty or humility; that others would reflect a greedy and foolish attitude to what one could expect out of life. Any of these examples may be disputed, but what is at issue is, should these difficult terms be there, or should the discussion be couched in terms that all clever adolescents can apply correctly? (Cf. the first half of the "major objection" above.)

Proceeding as it does in the virtue- and vice-related terms, the discussion thereby, inevitably, also contains claims about what is worthwhile, serious and important, good and evil, in our lives. So, for example, I claimed that parenthood is intrinsically worthwhile, and that having a good time was a worthless end (in life, not on individual occasions); that losing a fetus is always a serious matter (albeit not a tragedy in itself in the first trimester) whereas acquiring an appendectomy scar is a trivial one; that (human) death is an evil. Once again, these are difficult matters, and anyone might challenge any one of my claims. But what is at issue is, as before, should those difficult claims be there or can one reach practical conclusions about real moral issues that are in no way determined by premises about such matters? (Cf. the fifth criticism, and the second half of the "major criticism.")

The discussion also thereby, inevitably, contains claims about what life is like (e.g., my claim that love and friendship do not survive their parties' constantly insisting on their rights; or the claim that to demand perfection of life is to run the risk of missing out on happiness entirely). What is at issue is, should those disputable claims be there, or is our knowledge (or are our false opinions) about what life is like irrelevant to our understanding of real moral issues? (Cf. both halves of the "major criticism.")

Naturally, my own view is that all these concepts should be there in any discussion of real moral issues and that virtue theory, which uses all of them, is the right theory to apply to them. I do not pretend to have shown this. I realize that proponents of rival theories may say that, now that they have understood how virtue theory uses the range of concepts it draws on, they are more convinced than ever that such concepts should not figure in an adequate normative theory, because they are sectarian, or vague, or too particular, or improperly anthropocentric, and reinstate what I called the "major criticism." Or, finding many of the details of the discussion appropriate, they may agree that many, perhaps even all, of the concepts should figure, but argue that virtue theory gives an inaccurate account of the way the concepts fit together (and indeed of the concepts themselves) and that another theory provides a better account; that would be interesting to see. Moreover, I admitted that there were at least two problems for virtue theory: that it has to argue against moral skepticism, "pluralism," and cultural relativism, and that it has to find something to say about conflicting requirements of different virtues.

Proponents of rival theories might argue that their favored theory provides better solutions to these problems than virtue theory can. Indeed, they might criticize virtue theory for finding problems here at all. Anyone who argued for at least one of moral skepticism, "pluralism," or cultural relativism could presumably do so (provided their favored theory does not find a similar problem); and a utilitarian might say that benevolence is the only virtue and hence that virtue theory errs when it discusses even apparent conflicts between the requirements of benevolence and some other character trait such as honesty.

Defending virtue theory against all possible, or even likely, criticisms of it would be a lifelong task. As I said at the outset, in this article I aimed to defend the theory against some criticisms which I thought arose from an inadequate understanding of it, and to improve that understanding. If I have succeeded, we may hope for more comprehending criticisms of virtue theory than have appeared hitherto.

LYNN SHARP PAINE   Trade Secrets and the
                     Justification of
                     Intellectual Property:
                     A Comment on Hettinger

In a recent article Edwin Hettinger considers various rationales for recognizing intellectual property.[1] According to Hettinger, traditional justifications for property are especially problematic when applied to intellectual property because of its nonexclusive nature.[2] Since possessing and
using intellectual objects does not preclude their use and possession by
others, there is, he says, a "strong prima facie case against the wisdom
of private and exclusive intellectual property rights" (p. 35). There is,
moreover, a presumption against allowing restrictions on the free flow of
ideas (p. 51).

   After rejecting several rationales for intellectual property, Hettinger
finds its justification in an instrumental, or "utilitarian,"[3] argument
based on incentives (p. 47).[4] Respecting rights in ideas makes sense, he

   1. Edwin C. Hettinger, "Justifying Intellectual Property," *Philosophy & Public Affairs*
18, no. 1 (Winter 1989): 31–52. Subsequent page references to this article appear in pa-
rentheses in the text.
   2. Thomas Jefferson agrees. See Jefferson's letter to Isaac McPherson, 13 August 1813,
in *The Founder's Constitution*, ed. Philip B. Kurland and Ralph Lerner (Chicago: University of Chicago Press, 1987), 3:42.
   3. Hettinger uses the term *utilitarian* in a very narrow sense to refer to a justification
in terms of maximizing the use and dissemination of information. Some utilitarians might
see intellectual property institutions as promoting objectives other than information dissemination. My discussion of the roots of trade secret principles is perfectly consistent with
a utilitarian justification of those principles. Indeed, a utilitarian could argue (as many
economists do) that giving people certain rights in ideas they generate through their own
labor advances social well-being by promoting innovation. See, e.g., Robert U. Ayres,
"Technological Protection and Piracy: Some Implications for Policy," *Technological Fore-
casting and Social Change* 30 (1986): 5–18.
   4. In Hettinger's paper and in mine, the terms *justification, goal, purpose, rationale,*
and *objective* are used loosely and somewhat interchangeably. But, of course, identifying
the purpose or goal of our intellectual property institutions does not automatically justify

says, if we recognize that the purpose of our intellectual property institutions is to promote the dissemination and use of information (p. 49).
To the extent that existing institutions do not achieve this result, they
should be modified.[5] Skeptical about the effectiveness of current legal
arrangements, Hettinger concludes that we must think more imaginatively about structuring our intellectual property institutions—in particular, patent, copyright, and trade secret law—so that they increase the
availability and use of intellectual products. He ventures several possibilities for consideration: eliminating certain forms of trade secret protection, shortening the copyright and patent protection periods, and public
funding and ownership of intellectual objects (p. 49).

Hettinger's approach to justifying our intellectual property institutions
rests on several problematic assumptions. It assumes that all of our intellectual property institutions rise or fall together—that the rationale for

---

them. Some further legitimating idea or ultimate good, such as the general welfare or individual liberty, must be invoked. A difficulty with Hettinger's argument is that he identifies an objective for our intellectual property institutions—promoting the use and dissemination of ideas—and concludes that he has justified them. However, unless maximizing
the use and dissemination of ideas is an intrinsic good, we would expect a further step in
the argument linking this objective to an ultimate good. Hettinger may think this step can
be made or is self-evident from his terminology. However, it is not clear whether he calls
his justification "utilitarian" because of its consequentialist form or because he means to
appeal to social well-being or some particular good he associates with utilitarianism.

5. Hettinger seems to think that he has provided a clear-cut objective against which to
measure the effectiveness of our intellectual property institutions. Yet, a set of institutions
that maximized the "dissemination and use of information" (p. 49) would not necessarily
be most effective at "promoting the creation of valuable intellectual works" or promoting
" 'the progress of science and the useful arts' " (p. 47). A society might be quite successful
at disseminating information, but rather mediocre at creating valuable intellectual works.

There is an inevitable tension between the objectives of innovation and dissemination.
The same tension is present in other areas of law concerned with rights in information—
insider trading, for example. For discussion of this tension, see Frank H. Easterbrook, "Insider Trading, Secret Agents, Evidentiary Privileges, and the Production of Information,"
1981 Supreme Court Review, p. 309. While we struggle to piece together a system of information rights that gives due consideration to both objectives, we must be wary of the notion
that there is a single optimal allocation of rights.

Indeed, the very idea of a "socially optimal output of intellectual products" (p. 48) is
embarrassingly imprecise. What is a socially optimal output of poems, novels, computer
programs, movies, cassette recordings, production processes, formulations of matter, stock
tips, business strategies, etc.? How we allocate rights in ideas may affect the quality and
kinds of intellectual products that are produced as well as their quantity and dissemination.
Hettinger seems concerned primarily with quantity (p. 48). The use of general terms like
intellectual product and *socially optimal output* obscures the complexity of the empirical
assessment that Hettinger proposes.

trade secret protection must be the same as that for patent and copyright protection.[6] This assumption, I will try to show, is unwarranted. While it may be true that these institutions all promote social utility or well-being, the web of rights and duties understood under the general heading of "intellectual property rights" reflects a variety of more specific rationales and objectives.[7]

Second, Hettinger assumes that the rights commonly referred to as "intellectual property rights" are best understood on the model of rights in tangible and real property. He accepts the idea, implicit in the terminology, that intellectual property is like tangible property, only less corporeal (p. 31). This assumption leads him to focus his search for the justification of intellectual property on the traditional arguments for private property. I will try to show the merits of an alternative approach to thinking about rights in ideas—one that does not depend on the analogy with tangible property and that recognizes the role of ideas in defining personality and social relationships.

The combined effect of these assumptions is that trade secret law comes in for particularly serious criticism. It restricts methods of acquiring ideas (p. 35); it encourages secrecy (p. 36); it places unacceptable restrictions on employee mobility and technology transfer (p. 52); it can stifle competition (p. 50); it is more vulnerable to socialist objections (p. 52). In light of these deficiencies, Hettinger recommends that we consider the possibility of "eliminating most types of trade secrets entirely and letting patents carry a heavier load" (p. 49). He believes that trade secrets are undesirable in ways that copyrights and patents are not (p. 36).

6. Hettinger mentions trademark as another of our intellectual property institutions, along with our social sanction on plagiarism, but his central discussion focuses on copyright, patent, and trade secret concepts. Neither trademark principles nor the prohibition on plagiarism fits comfortably with his justification in terms of increasing the dissemination and use of ideas. Both are more closely related to giving recognition to the source or originator of ideas and products.

7. It may be helpful to think of two levels of justification: (1) an intermediate level consisting of objectives, purposes, reasons, and explanations for an institution or practice; and (2) an ultimate level linking those objectives and purposes to our most basic legitimating ideas such as the general good or individual liberty. Philosophers generally tend to be concerned with the ultimate level of justification while policymakers and judges more frequently operate at the intermediate level. Hettinger has, I think, mistaken an intermediate-level justification of patents and copyrights (promoting the dissemination and use of ideas) for an ultimate justification of intellectual property institutions.

Without disagreeing with Hettinger's recommendation that we re-evaluate and think more imaginatively about our intellectual property institutions, I believe we should have a clearer understanding of the various rationales for these institutions than is reflected in Hettinger's article. If we unbundle the notion of intellectual property into its constituent rights,[8] we find that different justifications are appropriate for different clusters of rights.[9] In particular, we find that the rights recognized by trade secret law are better understood as rooted in respect for individual liberty, confidential relationships, common morality, and fair competition than in the promotion of innovation and the dissemination of ideas. While trade secret law may serve some of the same ends as patent and copyright law, it has other foundations which are quite distinctive.[10]

In this article, I am primarily concerned with the foundations of trade secret principles. However, my general approach differs from Hettinger's in two fundamental ways. First, it focuses on persons and their relationships rather than property concepts. Second, it reverses the burden of justification, placing it on those who would argue for treating ideas as public goods rather than those who seek to justify private rights in ideas. Within this alternative framework, the central questions are how ideas may be legitimately acquired from others, how disclosure obligations arise, and how ideas become part of the common pool of knowledge. Be-

8. Hettinger, of course, recognizes that various rights are involved. He speaks of rights to possess, to personally use, to prevent others from using, to publish, and to receive the market value of one's ideas. And he notes that one might have a natural right to possess and personally use one's ideas even if one might not have a natural right to prevent others from copying them (p. 40). But he does not consider the possibility that the different rights involved in our concept of intellectual property may rest on quite varied foundations, some firmer than others.

9. It is generally accepted that the concept of property is best understood as a "bundle of rights." Just as the bundle of rights involved in home ownership differs substantially from the bundle of rights associated with stock ownership, the bundle of rights involved in patent protection differs from the bundle of rights involved in trade secret protection.

10. Today we commonly speak of copyright protection as providing incentives for intellectual effort, while at the same time ensuring widespread dissemination of ideas. As Hettinger notes, the effectiveness of copyright protection in achieving these aims may depend partly on the period of the copyright grant. Historically, at least before the first English copyright act, the famous 1710 Act of Anne, it appears that the dissemination of ideas was not so central. The common law gave the author an exclusive first right of printing or publishing her manuscript on the grounds that she was entitled to the product of her labor. The common law's position on the author's right to prohibit subsequent publication was less clear. See generally Wheaton v. Peters, 8 Pet. 591 (1834), reprinted in *The Founders' Constitution* 3:44–60.

fore turning to Hettinger's criticisms of trade secret principles, it will be useful to think more broadly about the rights of individuals over their undisclosed ideas. This inquiry will illustrate my approach to thinking about rights in ideas and point toward some of the issues at stake in the trade secret area.

The Right to Control Disclosure

If a person has any right with respect to her ideas, surely it is the right to control their initial disclosure.[11] A person may decide to keep her ideas to herself, to disclose them to a select few, or to publish them widely. Whether those ideas are best described as views and opinions, plans and intentions, facts and knowledge, or fantasies and inventions is immaterial. While it might in some cases be socially useful for a person to be generous with her ideas, and to share them with others without restraint, there is no general obligation to do so. The world at large has no right to the individual's ideas.[12]

Certainly, specific undertakings, relationships, and even the acquisition of specific information can give rise to disclosure obligations. Typically, these obligations relate to specific types of information pertinent to the relationship or the subject matter of the undertaking. A seller of goods must disclose to potential buyers latent defects and health and safety risks associated with the use of the goods. A person who undertakes to act as an agent for another is obliged to disclose to the principal information she acquires that relates to the subject matter of the agency. Disclosure obligations like these, however, are limited in scope and arise against a general background right to remain silent.

The right to control the initial disclosure of one's ideas is grounded in respect for the individual. Just as a person's sense of herself is intimately connected with the stream of ideas that constitutes consciousness, her public persona is determined in part by the ideas she expresses and the ways she expresses them. To require public disclosure of one's ideas and thoughts—whether about "personal" or other matters—would distort

11. Hettinger recognizes a right not to divulge privately created intellectual products (p. 46), but he does not fit this right into his discussion. If the right is taken seriously, however, it will, I believe, undermine Hettinger's own conclusions.

12. We would hope that the right to control disclosure would be exercised in a morally responsible way and that, for example, people with socially useful ideas would share them and that some types of harmful ideas would be withheld. But the potential social benefits of certain disclosures cannot justify a general requirement that ideas be disclosed.

one's personality and, no doubt, alter the nature of one's thoughts.[13] It would seriously interfere with the liberty to live according to one's chosen life plans. This sort of thought control would be an invasion of privacy and personality of the most intrusive sort. If anything is private, one's undisclosed thoughts surely are.[14]

Respect for autonomy, respect for personality, and respect for privacy lie behind the right to control disclosure of one's ideas, but the right is also part of what we mean by freedom of thought and expression. Frequently equated with a right to speak, freedom of expression also implies a prima facie right not to express one's ideas or to share them only with those we love or trust or with whom we wish to share.[15] These observations explain the peculiarity of setting up the free flow of ideas and unrestricted access as an ideal. Rights in ideas are desirable insofar as they strengthen our sense of individuality and undergird our social relationships. This suggests a framework quite different from Hettinger's, one that begins with a strong presumption against requiring disclosure and is in favor of protecting people against unconsented-to acquisitions of their ideas.[16] This is the moral backdrop against which trade secrecy law is best understood.

Consequences of Disclosure

Within this framework, a critical question is how people lose rights in their ideas. Are these rights forfeited when people express their ideas or communicate them to others? Surely this depends on the circumstances of disclosure. Writing down ideas in a daily journal to oneself or recording them on a cassette should not entail such a forfeiture. Considerations of individual autonomy, privacy, and personality require that such ex-

13. Here, I am using the term *personal* to refer to ideas about intimate matters, such as sexual behavior.

14. The right to control disclosure of one's thoughts might be thought to be no more than a reflection of technical limitations. Enforcing a general disclosure requirement presupposes some way of identifying the undisclosed thoughts of others. Currently, we do not have the technology to do this. But even if we did—or especially if we did—respect for the individual would preclude any form of monitoring people's thoughts.

15. On the relation between privacy and intimate relationships, see Charles Fried, "Privacy," *Yale Law Journal* 77 (1968): 475–93. Below, I will argue that confidentiality is central to other types of cooperative relationships as well.

16. Whether the presumption is overcome will depend on the importance of the objectives served by disclosure, and the degree of violence done to the individual or the relationship at stake.

pressions not be deemed available for use by others who may gain access to them.[17]

Likewise, communicating an idea in confidence to another should not render it part of the common pool of knowledge. Respect for the individual's desire to limit the dissemination of the idea is at stake, but so is respect for the relationship of trust and confidence among the persons involved. If A confides in B under circumstances in which B gives A reason to believe she will respect the confidence, A should be able to trust that B will not reveal or misuse the confidence and that third parties who may intentionally or accidentally discover the confidence will respect it.[18]

The alternative possibility is that by revealing her ideas to B, A is deemed to forfeit any right to control their use or communication. This principle is objectionable for a couple of reasons. First, it would most certainly increase reluctance to share ideas since our disclosure decisions are strongly influenced by the audience we anticipate. If we could not select our audience, that is, if the choice were only between keeping ideas to ourselves and sharing them with the world at large, many ideas would remain unexpressed, to the detriment of individual health as well as the general good.

Second, the principle would pose an impediment to the formation and sustenance of various types of cooperative relationships—relationships of love and friendship, as well as relationships forged for specific purposes such as education, medical care, or business. It might be thought that only ideas of an intimate or personal nature are important in this regard. But it is not only "personal" relationships, but cooperative relationships of all types, that are at stake. Shared knowledge and information of varying types are central to work relationships and communities—academic departments and disciplines, firms, teams—as well as other organizations. The possession of common ideas and information, to the exclusion of those outside the relationship or group, contributes to the group's self-definition and to the individual's sense of belonging. By permitting and protecting the sharing of confidences, trade secret principles, among other institutions, permit "special communities of knowledge" which

17. Technically, of course, others have access to ideas that have been expressed whereas they do not have access to undisclosed thoughts. But ease of access is not the criterion for propriety of access.

18. This is the fundamental principle behind the prohibition on insider trading.

nurture the social bonds and cooperative efforts through which we express our individuality and pursue common purposes.[19]

Of course, by disclosing her idea to B, A runs the risk that B or anyone else who learns about the idea may use it or share it further. But if B has agreed to respect the confidence, either explicitly or by participating in a relationship in which confidence is normally expected, she has a prima facie obligation not to disclose the information to which she is privy.[20] Institutions that give A a remedy against third parties who appropriate ideas shared in confidence reduce the risk that A's ideas will become public resources if she shares them with B. Such institutions thereby support confidential relationships and the cooperative undertakings that depend on them.

Yet another situation in which disclosure should not be regarded as a license for general use is the case of disclosures made as a result of deceit or insincere promises. Suppose A is an entrepreneur who has created an unusual software program with substantial sales potential. Another party, B, pretending to be a potential customer, questions A at great length about the code and other details of her program. A's disclosures are not intended to be, and should not be deemed, a contribution to the general pool of knowledge, nor should B be permitted to use A's ideas.[21] Respect for A's right to disclose her ideas requires that involuntary disclosures—such as those based on deceit, coercion, and theft of documents containing expressions of those ideas—not be regarded as forfeitures to the common pool of knowledge and information. In recognition of A's right to control disclosure of her ideas and to discourage appropriation of her ideas against her wishes, we might expect our institutions to provide A with a remedy against these sorts of appropriation. Trade secret law provides such a remedy.

Competitive fairness is also at stake if B is in competition with A. Besides having violated standards of common morality in using deceit to gain access to A's ideas, B is in a position to exploit those ideas in the marketplace without having contributed to the cost of their development.

19. The phrase "special communities of knowledge" comes from Kim Lane Scheppele, *Legal Secrets* (Chicago: University of Chicago Press, 1988), p. 14.

20. In practice, this prima facie obligation may sometimes be overridden when it conflicts with other obligations, e.g., the obligation to prevent harm to a third party.

21. An actual case similar to this was litigated in Pennsylvania. See Continental Data Systems, Inc. v. Exxon Corporation, 638 F. Supp. 432 (D.C.E.D. Pa. 1986).

B can sell her version of the software more cheaply since she enjoys a substantial cost advantage compared to A, who may have invested a great deal of time and money in developing the software. Fairness in a competitive economy requires some limitations on the rights of firms to use ideas developed by others. In a system based on effort, it is both unfair and ultimately self-defeating to permit firms to have a free ride on the efforts of their competitors.[22]

Problematic Issues

Respect for personal control over the disclosure of ideas, respect for confidential relationships, common morality, and fair competition all point toward recognizing certain rights in ideas. Difficult questions will arise within this system of rights. If A is not an individual but an organization or group, should A have the same rights and remedies against B or third parties who use or communicate information shared with B in confidence? For example, suppose A is a corporation that hires an employee, B, to develop a marketing plan. If other employees of A reveal in confidence to B information they have created or assembled, should A be able to restrain B from using this information to benefit herself (at A's expense)? Does it matter if A is a two-person corporation or a corporation with 100,000 employees? What if A is a social club or a private school?

Hettinger seems to assume that corporate A's should not have such rights—on the grounds that they might restrict B's employment possibilities. It is certainly true that giving A a right against B if she reveals information communicated to her in confidence could rule out certain jobs for B. However, the alternative rule—that corporate A's should have no rights in ideas they reveal in confidence to others—has problems as well.

One problem involves trust. If our institutions do not give corporate A's certain rights in ideas they reveal in confidence to employees, A's will seek other means of ensuring that competitively valuable ideas are protected. They may contract individually with employees for those rights, and if our legal institutions do not uphold those contracts, employers will seek to hire individuals in whom they have personal trust. Hiring would probably become more dependent on family and personal relationships

22. For the view that fair and honest business competition is the central policy underlying trade secret protection, see Ramon A. Klitzke, "Trade Secrets: Important Quasi-Property Rights," *Business Lawyer* 41 (1986): 557–70.

and there would be fewer opportunities for the less well connected. Institutional rules giving corporate A's rights against employees who reveal or use information given to them in confidence are a substitute for personal bonds of trust. While such rules are not cost-free and may have some morally undesirable consequences, they help sustain cooperative efforts and contribute to more open hiring practices.

Contrary to Hettinger's suggestion, giving corporate A's rights in the ideas they reveal in confidence to others does not always benefit the strong at the expense of the weak, or the large corporation at the expense of the individual, although this is surely sometimes the case.[23] Imagine three entrepreneurs who wish to expand their highly successful cookie business. A venture capitalist interested in financing the expansion naturally wishes to know the details of the operation—including the prized cookie recipe—before putting up capital. After examining the recipe, however, he decides that it would be more profitable for him to sell the recipe to CookieCo, a multinational food company, and to invest his capital elsewhere. Without money and rights to prevent others from using the recipe, the corporate entrepreneurs are very likely out of business. CookieCo, which can manufacture and sell the cookies much more cheaply, will undoubtedly find that most of the entrepreneurs' customers are quite happy to buy the same cookies for less at their local supermarket.

Non-Property Foundations of Trade Secret Law

To a large extent, the rights and remedies mentioned in the preceding discussion are those recognized by trade secret law. As this discussion showed, the concept of property is not necessary to justify these rights. Trade secret law protects against certain methods of appropriating the confidential and commercially valuable ideas of others. It affords a remedy to those whose commercially valuable secrets are acquired by misrepresentation, theft, bribery, breach or inducement of a breach of confidence, espionage, or other improper means.[24] Although the roots of

23. It appears that Hettinger is using the term *private company* in contrast to individuals rather than to public companies—those whose shares are sold to the public on national stock exchanges. If one wishes to protect individuals, however, it might be more important to distinguish small, privately held companies from large, publicly held ones than to distinguish individuals from companies. Many individuals, however, are dependent on large, publicly held companies for their livelihood.

24. *Uniform Trade Secrets Act with 1985 Amendments*, sec. 1, in *Uniform Laws Annotated*, vol. 14 (1980 with 1988 Pocket Part). The Uniform Trade Secrets Act seeks to codify

trade secret principles have been variously located, respect for voluntary disclosure decisions and respect for confidential relationships provide the best account of the pattern of permitted and prohibited appropriations and use of ideas.[25] As Justice Oliver Wendell Holmes noted in a 1917 trade secret case, "The property may be denied but the confidence cannot be."[26] Trade secret law can also be seen as enforcing ordinary standards of morality in commercial relationships, thus ensuring some consistency with general social morality.[27]

It may well be true, as Hettinger and others have claimed, that the availability of trade secret protection provides an incentive for intellectual labor and the development of ideas. The knowledge that they have legal rights against those who "misappropriate" their ideas may encourage people to invest large amounts of time and money in exploring and developing ideas. However, the claim that trade secret protection promotes invention is quite different from the claim that it is grounded in or justified by this tendency. Even if common law trade secret rights did not promote intellectual labor or increase the dissemination and use of information, there would still be reasons to recognize those rights. Respect for people's voluntary disclosure decisions, respect for confidential relationships, standards of common morality, and fair competition would still point in that direction.

Moreover, promoting the development of ideas cannot be the whole story behind trade secret principles, since protection is often accorded to information such as customer data or cost and pricing information kept in the ordinary course of doing business. While businesses may need incentives to engage in costly research and development, they would certainly keep track of their customers and costs in any event. The rationale for giving protection to such information must be other than promoting

---

and standardize the common law principles of trade secret law as they have developed in different jurisdictions.

25. See Klitzke, "Trade Secrets." Different theories of justification are discussed in Ridsdale Ellis, *Trade Secrets* (New York: Baker, Voorhis, 1953). Kim Lane Scheppele is another commentator favoring the view that breach of confidence is what trade secret cases are all about. See *Legal Secrets*, p. 241. In their famous article on privacy, Warren and Brandeis find the roots of trade secret principles in the right to privacy. Samuel D. Warren and Louis D. Brandeis, *Harvard Law Review* 4 (1890): 212.

26. E. I. DuPont de Nemours Powder Co. v. Masland, 244 U.S. 100 (1917).

27. One commentator has said, "The desire to reinforce 'good faith and honest, fair dealing' in business is the mother of the law of trade secrets." Russell B. Stevenson, Jr., *Corporations and Information* (Baltimore: Johns Hopkins University Press, 1980), p. 19.

the invention, dissemination, and use of ideas. By the same token, trade secret principles do not prohibit the use of ideas acquired by studying products available in the marketplace. If the central policy behind trade secret protection were the promotion of invention, one might expect that trade secret law, like patent law, which was explicitly fashioned to encourage invention, would protect innovators from imitators.

The fact that Congress has enacted patent laws giving inventors a limited monopoly in exchange for disclosure of their ideas without at the same time eliminating state trade secret law may be a further indication that trade secret and patent protection rest on different grounds.[28] By offering a limited monopoly in exchange for disclosure, the patent laws implicitly recognize the more fundamental right not to disclose one's ideas at all or to disclose them in confidence to others.[29]

Reassessing Hettinger's Criticisms of Trade Secret Law
If we see trade secret law as grounded in respect for voluntary disclosure, confidential relationships, common morality, and fair competition, the force of Hettinger's criticisms diminishes somewhat. The problems he cites appear not merely in their negative light as detracting from an ideal "free flow of ideas," but in their positive role as promoting other important values.

a. Restrictions on Acquiring Ideas. Hettinger is critical, for example, of the fact that trade secret law restricts methods of acquiring ideas. But the prohibited means of acquisition—misrepresentation, theft, bribery, breach of confidence, and espionage—all reflect general social morality. Lifting these restrictions would undoubtedly contribute to the erosion of important values outside the commercial context.

How much trade secrecy laws inhibit the development and spread of ideas is also open to debate. Hettinger and others have claimed that trade secrecy is a serious impediment to innovation and dissemination because the period of permitted secrecy is unlimited. Yet, given the fact that trade secret law offers no protection for ideas acquired by examining or re-

28. Support for this interpretation is found in Justice Thurgood Marshall's concurring opinion in Kewanee Oil Co. v. Bicron Corp., 416 U.S. 470, 494 (1974). The court held that the federal patent laws do not preempt state trade secret laws.

29. Congress may have realized that trying to bring about more openness by eliminating trade secret protection, even with the added attraction of a limited monopoly for inventions that qualify for patent protection, would be inconsistent with fundamental moral notions such as respect for confidential relationships, and would probably not have worked anyway.

verse-engineering products in the marketplace, it would appear rather
difficult to maintain technical secrets embodied in those products while
still exploiting their market potential. A standard example used to illustrate the problem of perpetual secrecy, the Coke formula, seems insuffi-
cient to establish that this is a serious problem. Despite the complexity
of modern technology, successful reverse-engineering is common. Moreover, similar technical advances are frequently made by researchers
working independently. Trade secret law poses no impediment in either
case. Independent discoverers are free to exploit their ideas even if they
are similar to those of others.

As for nontechnical information such as marketing plans and business
strategies, the period of secrecy is necessarily rather short since imple-
mentation entails disclosure. Competitor intelligence specialists claim
that most of the information needed to understand what competitors are
doing is publicly available.[30] All of these considerations suggest that
trade secret principles are not such a serious impediment to the dissemination of information.

b. Competitive Effects. Hettinger complains that trade secret principles stifle competition. Assessing this claim is very difficult. On one
hand, it may seem that prices would be lower if firms were permitted to
obtain cost or other market advantages by using prohibited means to acquire protected ideas from others. Competitor access to the Coke formula
would most likely put downward pressure on the price of "the real thing."
Yet, it is also reasonable to assume that the law keeps prices down by
reducing the costs of self-protection. By giving some assurance that commercially valuable secrets will be protected, the law shields firms from
having to bear the full costs of protection. It is very hard to predict what
would happen to prices if trade secret protection were eliminated. Self-
protection would be more costly and would tend to drive prices up, while
increased competition would work in the opposite direction. There would
surely be important differences in morale and productivity. Moreover, as
noted, any price reductions for consumers would come at a cost to the
basic moral standards of society if intelligence-gathering by bribery, misrepresentation, and espionage were permitted.

30. See, e.g., the statement of a manager of a competitor surveillance group quoted in
Jerry L. Wall, "What the Competition Is Doing: Your Need to Know," *Harvard Business
Review* 52 (November–December 1974): 34. See generally Leonard M. Fuld, *Competitor
Intelligence: How to Get It—How to Use It* (New York: John Wiley and Sons, 1985).

c. Restrictions on Employee Mobility. Among Hettinger's criticisms of trade secret law, the most serious relate to restrictions on employee mobility. In practice, employers often attempt to protect information by overrestricting the postemployment opportunities of employees. Three important factors contribute to this tendency: vagueness about which information is confidential; disagreement about the proper allocation of rights to ideas generated by employees using their employers' resources; and conceptual difficulties in distinguishing general knowledge and employer-specific knowledge acquired on the job. Courts, however, are already doing what Hettinger recommends, namely, limiting the restrictions that employers can place on future employment in the name of protecting ideas.[31] Although the balance between employer and employee interests is a delicate one not always equitably struck, the solution of eliminating trade secret protection altogether is overbroad and undesirable, considering the other objectives at stake.

d. Hypothetical Alternatives. Hettinger's discussion of our intellectual property institutions reflects an assumption that greater openness and sharing would occur if we eliminated trade secret protection. He argues that trade secret principles encourage secrecy. He speaks of the "free flow of ideas" as the ideal that would obtain in the absence of our intellectual property institutions. This supposition strikes me as highly unlikely. People keep secrets and establish confidential relationships for a variety of reasons that are quite independent of any legal protection these secrets might have. The psychology and sociology of secrets have been explored by others. Although much economic theory is premised on complete information, secrecy and private information are at the heart of day-to-day competition in the marketplace.

In the absence of something like trade secret principles, I would expect not a free flow of ideas but greater efforts to protect information through contracts, management systems designed to limit information access, security equipment, and electronic counterintelligence devices. I would also expect stepped-up efforts to acquire intelligence from others through espionage, bribery, misrepresentation, and other unsavory means. By providing some assurance that information can be shared in confidence and by protecting against unethical methods of extracting in-

---

31. See, e.g., John Burgess, "Unlocking Corporate Shackles," *Washington Business*, 11 December 1989, p. 1.

formation and undermining confidentiality, trade secret principles promote cooperation and security, two important conditions for intellectual endeavor. In this way, trade secret principles may ultimately promote intellectual effort by limiting information flow.

The Burden of Justification

We may begin thinking about information rights, as Hettinger does, by treating all ideas as part of a common pool and then deciding whether and how to allocate to individuals rights to items in the pool. Within this framework, ideas are conceived on the model of tangible property.[32] Just as, in the absence of social institutions, we enter the world with no particular relationship to its tangible assets or natural resources, we have no particular claim on the world's ideas. In this scheme, as Hettinger asserts, the "burden of justification is very much on those who would restrict the maximal use of intellectual objects" (p. 35).

Alternatively, we may begin, as I do, by thinking of ideas in relation to their originators, who may or may not share their ideas with specific others or contribute them to the common pool. This approach treats ideas as central to personality and the social world individuals construct for themselves. Ideas are not, in the first instance, freely available natural resources. They originate with people, and it is the connections among people, their ideas, and their relationships with others that provides a baseline for discussing rights in ideas. Within this conception, the burden of justification is on those who would argue for disclosure obligations and general access to ideas.

The structure of specific rights that emerges from these different frameworks depends not only on where the burden of justification is located, but also on how easily it can be discharged.[33] It is unclear how compelling a case is required to overcome the burden Hettinger sets up and, consequently, difficult to gauge the depth of my disagreement with him.[34] Since Hettinger does not consider the rationales for trade secret

---

32. Hettinger speaks of ideas as objects, and of rights in ideas as comparable to water or mineral rights. Indeed, according to Hettinger, the difficulty in justifying intellectual property rights arises because ideas are not in all respects like tangible property, which he thinks is more easily justified.

33. The Editors of *Philosophy & Public Affairs* encouraged me to address this point.

34. His argument from maximizing the production and dissemination of ideas suggests that the presumption in favor of free ideas is not terribly strong: it can be overridden by identifying some reasonable objective likely to be served by assigning exclusive rights.

principles discussed here, it is not clear whether he would dismiss them altogether, find them insufficiently weighty to override the presumption he sets up, or agree that they satisfy the burden of justification.

One might suspect, however, from the absence of discussion of the personal and social dimension of rights in ideas that Hettinger does not think them terribly important, and that his decision to put the burden of justification on those who argue for rights in ideas reflects a fairly strong commitment to openness. On the assumption that our alternative starting points reflect seriously held substantive views (they are not just procedural devices to get the argument started) and that both frameworks require strong reasons to overcome the initial presumption, the resulting rights and obligations are likely to be quite different in areas where neither confidentiality nor openness is critical to immediate human needs. Indeed, trade secrecy law is an area where these different starting points would be likely to surface.

The key question to ask about these competing frameworks is which is backed by stronger reasons. My opposition to Hettinger's allocation of the burden of justification rests on my rejection of his conception of ideas as natural resources and on different views of how the world would look in the absence of our intellectual property institutions. In contrast, my starting point acknowledges the importance of ideas to our sense of ourselves and the communities (including work communities) of which we are a part. It is also more compatible with the way we commonly talk about ideas. Our talk about disclosure obligations presupposes a general background right not to reveal ideas. If it were otherwise, we would speak of concealment rights. To use the logically interesting feature of nonexclusiveness as a starting point for moral reasoning about rights in ideas seems wholly arbitrary.

Conclusion

Knives, forks, and spoons are all designed to help us eat. In a sense, however, the essential function of these tools is to help us cut, since without utensils, we could still consume most foods with our hands. One might be tempted to say that since cutting is the essential function of eating utensils, forks and spoons should be designed to facilitate cutting. One might even say that insofar as forks and spoons do not facilitate cutting, they should be redesigned. Such a modification, however, would rob us of valuable specialized eating instruments.

Hettinger's train of thought strikes me as very similar. He purports to examine the justification of our various intellectual property institutions. However, he settles on a justification that really only fits patent and, arguably, copyright institutions. He then suggests that other intellectual property rights be assessed against the justification he proposes and redesigned insofar as they are found wanting. In particular, he suggests that trade secret principles be modified to look more like patent principles. Hettinger fails to appreciate the various rationales behind the rights and duties understood under the heading "intellectual property," especially those recognized by trade secret law.

I agree with Hettinger that our intellectual property institutions need a fresh look from a utilitarian perspective.[35] The seventeen-year monopoly granted through patents is anachronistic given the pace of technological development today. We need to think about the appropriate balance between employer and employee rights in ideas developed jointly. Solutions to the problem of the unauthorized copying of software may be found in alternative pricing structures rather than in fundamental modifications of our institutions. Public interest considerations could be advanced for opening access to privately held information in a variety of areas. As we consider these specific questions, however, I would urge that we keep firmly in mind the variety of objectives that intellectual property institutions have traditionally served.[36] If, following Hettinger's advice, we single-mindedly reshape these institutions to maximize the short-term dissemination and use of ideas, we run the risk of subverting the other ends these institutions serve.

35. That is, we should look at the effects of these institutions on social well-being in general and select the institutions that are best on the whole.

36. A utilitarian assessment will also include consideration of the various interests that would be affected by alternative allocations of intellectual property rights. For example, denying authors copyright in their works may increase the power and profit of publishers and further impair the ability of lesser-known writers to find publication outlets. One scholar has concluded that America's failure to recognize the copyrights of aliens before 1891 stunted the development of native literature. For fifty years before the passage of the Platt-Simmonds Act, publishing interests vigorously and successfully opposed recognition of international copyright. This is understandable since the works of well-known British authors were available to publishers free of charge. Publishers were not terribly concerned with the artistic integrity of these works. They sometimes substituted alternative endings, mixed the works of different authors, and edited as economically necessary. There were few reasons to take the risks involved in publishing the works of unknown and untested American writers who might insist on artistic integrity. See generally Aubert J. Clark, *The Movement for International Copyright in Nineteenth Century America* (Westport, Conn.: Greenwood Press, 1973).

ALLAN GIBBARD   Constructing Justice

Brian Barry's *Treatise on Social Justice* is to comprise three volumes. Such a literary undertaking has an olden feel, but the characters are mostly in modern dress, and they help themselves to modern devices. Volume 1 is now at hand, and in it we see two great rival theories step forward to vie for the hand of Justice. Mutual Advantage is a theory with sterling qualities, but in him too we note substantial flaws. We get to know him well; he is treated with elaborate consideration, and provided with enough rope to hang himself. Impartiality is the nobler of the two, and though we come to know his ways less thoroughly, he survives with honor intact to play the lead role in the forthcoming volumes 2 and 3.

Justice as Mutual Advantage, explains Barry, consists in "the constraints on themselves that rational self-interested people would agree to as the minimum price that has to be paid in order to obtain the cooperation of others." Justice, then, "is simply rational prudence pursued in contexts where the cooperation (or at least forbearance) of other people is a condition of our being able to get what we want." Plato took this as the theory to beat, and so does Barry. Barry, though, says he hopes to give it "a better run for its money than it got from Plato" (pp. 6–7).

Justice as Impartiality is "less conceptually parsimonious." The reason for behaving justly, on this view, "is not reducible to even a sophisticated and indirect pursuit of self-interest." The motive for just conduct is, rather, "the desire to act in ways that can be defended to oneself and others without appealing to personal advantage." This, Barry says, is an original principle of human nature (pp. 7–8, 361–64).

A review of Brian Barry, *Theories of Justice* (Berkeley and Los Angeles: University of California Press, 1989). Parenthetical page references are to this book.

Justice as Mutual Advantage is coherent, Barry thinks, but wrong: we cannot recognize it as all of justice. Justice redresses bargaining advantages, whereas Justice as Mutual Advantage threatens merely to smooth the path of exploitation. True justice is Justice as Impartiality.

In a running subplot, mathematical game theory plays Barber of Seville to both rivals, proffering the most ingenious help—but in the end it fails to gain for itself a secure lackeyhood in the castle of justice. A great current hope in moral theory has been that modern, technical game theory could be put to moral use. Game theory beautifully captures various insights of Hobbes and Hume. The hope is to use it to formulate precise moral theories that capture these insights, theories with powerful rationales powerfully displayed. A recurrent stratagem in this enterprise has been *constructivist*: The theorist specifies an ideal, hypothetical situation in which people choose the principles that shall govern them. He then proclaims that whatever principles would be chosen in that situation are, by virtue of this very fact, valid principles of justice. What the ideal situation is to be like is hotly disputed: Harsanyi and Rawls have self-interested parties behind a veil of ignorance; Gauthier has self-interested agents who know their bargaining advantages and use them to the hilt.[1] Still, with any version of this program, the hope is that precise theories of self-interested bargaining and choice will yield precise conclusions about justice. Barry calls this *hard constructivism*. We can think of this first volume as a painstaking rejection of hard constructivism in all of its forms.

Barry too is a constructivist, but, as he puts it, a *soft* constructivist. He agrees that we learn valid principles of justice by considering a hypothetical choice of principles. The parties who do the choosing, though, must not be purely self-interested. They are "reasonable"—a term that has moral content. When asked to say what is reasonable in this morally laden sense, technical game theory stands mute.

Brian Barry is a grand master of normative political theory, and the best course for a discussant might well be uncritical adulation. Barry is unmatched in his knowledge of this field, and he is dogged, incisive, judicious, and insightful. Indeed, when we learn more in the next vol-

---

1. John Harsanyi, "Cardinal Utility in Welfare Economics and in the Theory of Risk-Taking," *Journal of Political Economy* 61 (1953): 434–35; John Rawls, *A Theory of Justice* (Cambridge, Mass.: Harvard University Press, 1971); and David Gauthier, *Morals by Agreement* (Oxford: Oxford University Press, 1986).

ume about what Justice as Impartiality is, we may well find to boot that Barry is right: that Justice as Impartiality is the best interpretation of justice. Still, in the wake of Barry's harvest I glean a few doubts worth threshing. Barry, I think, may dismiss too easily an important alternative conception of justice, the one Rawls has called Justice as Reciprocity. As for Justice as Mutual Advantage, Barry may give it more of a run for its money than it merits. And Justice as Impartiality may be too vague to be a clear, distinct alternative.

I. THE MOTIVE OF FAIR RECIPROCITY

Barry treats John Rawls as hovering uneasily between the two perches Barry identifies—between impartiality and mutual advantage. Perhaps he is right in this, but Rawls long ago seemed to have his eye on a third perch: one he called Justice as Reciprocity. Whether Rawls had identified a coherent, distinct alternative is unclear, but let me pursue the case that he had.

If I return favor for favor, I may be doing so in pursuit of my own advantage, as a means to keep the favors rolling. My motivation might, though, be more intrinsically reciprocal: I might be decent to him because he has been decent to me. I might prefer treating another well who has treated me well, even if he has no further power to affect me. We tip for good service in strange restaurants.

Reciprocity needs terms of trade: we exchange unlikes, and we can ask what makes the exchange fair or unfair. Rawls proposes that justice is fairness in exchange, but on a grand scale: it is fairness in the terms governing a society-wide system of reciprocity. The system consists in each person's supporting a basic social structure and drawing benefits from it. The citizen of a well-ordered society is motivated to return benefits fairly, and this general motivation becomes a motivation to conform to the rules of a social structure he considers fair.

Is Justice as Fair Reciprocity a distinct alternative to Barry's two? Is it different in any way from Justice as Mutual Advantage and Justice as Impartiality? The case that it is, in a nutshell, is this: On the one hand, it is distinct from Justice as Mutual Advantage because it draws on non-egoistic motives. On the other, it is distinct from Justice as Impartiality because it says that a person cannot reasonably be asked to support a social order unless he gains from it.

Take first Mutual Advantage. Motivations of reciprocity are not purely egoistic. David Gauthier, to be sure, embraces fair reciprocity as a dictate of mutual advantage.[2] Intrinsic motivations of reciprocity constitute a part of rational prudence, Gauthier claims, a part of the rational pursuit of one's own interest. It is selfishly rational to tip the waiter you will never see again. Why? Because if you had been the sort of person who would not tip, he could have seen it in your face and would not have given you good service.

Many commentators on Gauthier, however, have been unpersuaded by this part of his argument. Much depends, first, on just how hard it is for a cad to put on an honest face. Some, alas, seem to manage it quite well. Second, even if you cannot keep a straight face, what that shows is not that true honor and decency constitute rational prudence. It shows that it could be rationally prudent to cultivate a nature that disposes one, at times, to depart from rational prudence. If these criticisms are right, motives of fair reciprocity cannot be reduced to motives of prudence. Justice as Fair Reciprocity is not a version of Justice as Mutual Advantage.[3]

Turn now to Justice as Impartiality, which celebrates a nonegoistic motivation to be just. "The motive for behaving justly is, on this view, the desire to act in accordance with principles that could not reasonably be rejected by people seeking an agreement with others under conditions free from morally irrelevant bargaining advantages and disadvantages" (p. 8).[4] The just person is moved to adhere to an agreement that is acceptable from all points of view. Is this any different from wanting to reciprocate fairly? Fair reciprocity, after all, requires a standard of fairness in exchanges. Justice as Impartiality might provide the standard. Perhaps fair terms of reciprocity are whatever terms every reasonable person would find acceptable.

In Barry's arguments for Justice as Impartiality, however, he rejects the very features of Rawls's treatment that most characterize it as a version of Justice as Fair Reciprocity. Rawls treats society as "a cooperative scheme for mutual advantage," and the mutual advantage is in compar-

2. See esp. *Morals by Agreement.*

3. Cf. Allen Buchanan, "Justice as Reciprocity versus Subject-Centered Justice," *Philosophy & Public Affairs* 19, no. 3 (Summer 1990): 230.

4. This motive and this test for principles were formulated in T. M. Scanlon, "Contractualism and Utilitarianism," in *Utilitarianism and Beyond*, ed. Amartya Sen and Bernard Williams (Cambridge: Cambridge University Press, 1982), pp. 103–28.

ison to a benchmark of general egoism. This comparison with a noncooperative benchmark of nonagreement is no part of Justice as Impartiality as Barry conceives it. Barry, indeed, argues that the benchmark is out of spirit with various other commitments of Rawls's. I myself do not think the case is clear-cut, and I shall sketch a case for the coherence of much of Rawls's approach.

Natural and social advantages are morally arbitrary. Rawls stresses this, and Barry agrees heartily. Now these considerations, argues Barry against Rawls, discredit Justice as Fair Reciprocity. We must reject "the justice of inequalities based on morally arbitrary advantages" (p. 239). That means we cannot treat society as a "cooperative venture for mutual advantage," for in the course of setting the terms of such a venture, each party brings his natural advantages and disadvantages to the bargaining table. That skews the outcome unjustly (pp. 234–35).

Barry no more than Rawls, though, outright rejects "the justice of inequalities based on morally arbitrary advantages." Rawls's difference principle allows for inequalities, so long as they are to the benefit of the worst-off, and Barry does not object. Any inequalities that flow from a social order will have causes, and Rawls agrees with Barry in thinking that the ultimate causes must be morally arbitrary. Neither concludes from this that all such inequalities are unjust.

At other times Barry puts his point far more tenably. "The central issue in any theory of justice is the defensibility of unequal relations between people" (p. 3). Equality needs no justification, whereas departures from it do. The point about the moral arbitrariness of endowments, then, concerns justification. Differing natural and social endowments do not by themselves justify unequal outcomes. If it is just that unequal endowments lead to unequal outcomes, that must be because the social structure that lets this happen is just—and in arguing that the social structure is just, we cannot assume at the outset that unequal endowments give rise to unequal desert or entitlements.

Now this point seems correct to me, and important—and it can, sure enough, be combined with Barry's default preference for equality. Still, the points are separate. The moral arbitrariness of natural and social endowments in itself places no prior restriction on ways desert and entitlement can justly be affected by these endowments—as property entitlements are under Rawls's difference principle. The point is, if we claim that there is such a dependence, this claim needs to be justified.

For all this tells us, we can still regard society as a joint venture for mutual advantage. The prime question Rawls addresses might be not "Why accept inequality?" but "Why limit myself in pursuit of my own advantage?" This is a question that can be asked also by a well-off person: he has much, but why not go for more? Rawls, in effect, gives this answer: "You have what you have only because others constrain themselves, in ways that make for a fair cooperative venture for mutual advantage. Constrain yourself by those rules in return, and you give them fair return for what they give you." Whether this answer moves a person depends on his sentiments of fair reciprocity.

Suppose each person sprang into existence on a separate island, adult and able. Each produced independently, and each was protected by the water from threats and from takings. Even then, Barry holds, equal division would prima facie be required by justice. If some islands were fertile and others barren, the difference would be morally arbitrary. The lucky ones, then, would be required by considerations of justice to share (pp. 238–39).[5]

So argues Barry, and perhaps he is right. Still, from the bare assumption that fertility is morally arbitrary, no obligation to share follows. The lucky ones could admit that their luck is morally arbitrary, and still ask "Why share?" One answer they could not be given is that sharing pays others back for their cooperation or their restraint. No one has cooperated and no one has restrained himself, and so there is nothing to pay back. Motives of fair reciprocity, then, would not lead the lucky ones to share, even though they freely admitted that their luck was morally arbitrary.

II. The Content of Fair Reciprocity

Could Rawls's difference principle be accepted by people whose moral motivations are ones of fair reciprocity? Could it be accepted as giving fair terms of reciprocity in society conceived as a venture for mutual advantage? Barry thinks not. Fair terms, so conceived, should be not only mutually advantageous, but advantageous to an equal degree. "To be stable, in other words, the solution should reflect the bargaining power of

5. See Robert Nozick, *Anarchy, State, and Utopia* (New York: Basic Books, 1974), p. 185, and Gauthier, *Morals by Agreement*, pp. 218–19.

the parties." This requirement yields not the difference principle, but something more inegalitarian. "Introducing the requirement of mutual advantage threatens to unravel Rawls's theory" (p. 249).

Now perhaps fair reciprocity does require equal advantage for all, as Barry maintains. This would mean equal advantage as measured from the "disagreement point," meaning the situation that would obtain if no agreement were reached. If the disagreement point relevant to the social contract made some people quite well off and others quite badly off, then sentiments of fair reciprocity might endorse preserving this inequality. Perhaps—though it must be psychologically contingent what terms of social exchange will be seen as fair. In truth, though, a disagreement point of general egoism would be highly egalitarian. In a world where life is short, nasty, and brutish for all, could there be much difference in prospects for misery, compared to the gains to be had from cooperation and mutual restraint? Even the strongest is easily killed. We are tempted to think that if a native quality is fortunate for a person in an orderly market society, it must be a godsend to him in a state of nature. Barry himself, though, points out that a "brilliant but severely handicapped person may do very well in a market society" (p. 253), though he would starve in a world without nurture, education, and protection. Strength and guile we imagine to be useful anywhere, but they may put one in deadly competition with others who also have guile if not strength.[6]

Gauthier appears to draw inegalitarian conclusions from bargaining considerations, but as Barry notes, the conclusions depend on a bizarre choice of disagreement point. Gauthier's bargaining proceeds not from a state of general egoism, but from an idyllic (for the lucky) market economy—a Lockean world, except that whereas Locke thought that rules of property would need enforcement, and that enforcement would lead to quarrels and fighting, the market constraints of Gauthier's disagreement point are enforced as if by magic. Why should anyone starve peaceably

6. The notion of a disagreement point for the social contract may be puzzling. It is not to be a breakdown into warring subgroups, as in recent years in Lebanon. For then each subgroup has elements of a social contract, whereas the disagreement point is to be life without a social contract at all. Moreover, when a social contract breaks down, people still have characteristics formed under old arrangements. Part of what we reciprocate under a social contract is the cooperation and mutual restraint that allowed our nurture and formation. Should the relevant disagreement point, then, be one in which we are all dead as babies? Should it be like Rousseau's state of nature, with each person solitary and animal-like? It is hard to say—but in any case, it will be bad, and roughly equally bad for everyone.

just because he would do badly in a Lockean world with magic police? (Gauthier has answers; Barry and I both find them unconvincing.)[7]

Gauthier awards the person who gains least the most gain possible, where gain is measured from Gauthier's strangely chosen disagreement point. As for the unit of gain, it is the gain that would come if the entire surplus derivable from cooperation were awarded to that person.[8] Call this each person's *maximum gain*. Maximum gain is insensitive to productive abilities; if everyone works for you, why work yourself? Roughly, we can say this: If Gauthier's disagreement point were one of general egoism and not of Lockean magic, everyone's state at the disagreement point would be about the same. Roughly, too, everyone's state of maximum gain is the same. To maximize the gain of the one who gains least is to make the worst-off as well off as possible—the requirement of Rawls's difference principle. Fix up Gauthier's disagreement point, and from his theory out pops Rawls.[9]

Still, not all is well with Justice as Fair Reciprocity—for reasons laid out recently by Allen Buchanan.[10] The great fly in the ointment is exclusion.[11] The rationale for being just, on this conception, is that one gives fair return to others by supporting a society-wide scheme of fair reciprocity. Who gets included in the scheme? Nothing in this bare rationale tells us. There are good egoistic reasons for including anyone who would make too much trouble otherwise. But if outsiders can be controlled at small enough cost without invoking their voluntary restraint, must they be offered fair terms?

Barry argues that because of the possibility of exclusion, a require-

7. See Gauthier, *Morals by Agreement*, pp. 190–221, and Barry, pp. 249–54.

8. Gauthier, *Morals by Agreement*, pp. 113–56.

9. Gauthier's theory employs utilities, whereas Rawls uses primary social goods: things such as money, powers, and opportunities that it is rational to want whatever else one wants. This difference, though, should not much affect the present argument. In a state of nature, whether Hobbes's or Rousseau's, primary social goods are grievously lacking for all. On the other hand, anyone who could pocket the entire social surplus would have primary social goods without practical limit. In terms of primary social goods, then, each person's allotment is roughly equal to everyone else's at the disagreement point, and each person's maximum gain is equal to everyone else's. Thus unless there are great differences in the broad shapes of people's utility curves connecting these two extreme points, this should translate, by Gauthier's theory of maximin relative utility gains, into a maximin distribution of prospects for primary social goods—Rawls's difference principle.

10. Buchanan, "Justice as Reciprocity."

11. Ibid., esp. pp. 250–51.

ment of mutual advantage has the following strong consequence: "Justice is done when the distribution of income is such that *there is no coalition that could do better for itself economically by withdrawing with a per-capita equal share of the society's nonhuman productive assets*—capital, goods, natural resources, etc." (p. 243; italics mine).[12] I myself think that this is wrong, and indeed that it repeats a mistake of Gauthier's. It is not only cooperation that is at stake in questions of justice, but mutual restraint: nonaggression and respect for a system of property rights. Just people forgo chances to seize advantage, and the idea of Justice as Fair Reciprocity is that they forgo these chances in return for others' voluntary support of just arrangements. Now a coalition that withdraws from society renounces any claim to justice from those who remain. Why think they could take along their per capita share of nonhuman productive assets? Why think they could avoid slavery at the hands of everyone else? Why think they could keep the product of their labor and capital? To claim Justice as Fair Reciprocity, one must offer fair reciprocity.

The real sources of worry that Barry identifies are, I think, these two: First, groups incapable of voluntary restraint in accordance with standards of justice. Animals and some of the feebleminded are incapable of having their actions guided by standards of justice. Some congenitally handicapped people can be ignored as incapable either of contribution or disruption. Babies may reciprocate someday if they live, but could be tortured to death without violating demands of fair reciprocity. Future generations cannot directly affect the living.[13] Rawls finds himself forced to treat these all as separate problems. Perhaps he is right: fair reciprocity is not everything, but still it is crucial to many types of social cooperation. Its content needs to be elucidated. Barry, though, hopes for a conception of justice that admits these cases as central.

A second, worse worry is helotry—and this bullet would be harder to bite. What if a group can be enslaved without excuses, and enslaved profitably? The group is excluded from the terms of voluntary cooperation

12. As Barry notes, this standard is developed by John Roemer, *A General Theory of Exploitation and Class* (Cambridge, Mass.: Harvard University Press, 1982), esp. chap. 7. It avoids "capitalist exploitation," Roemer says, but is still inadequate.

13. Rawls gives different treatments of these various problems. See *A Theory of Justice*, p. 509, on infants; p. 512 on animals; and pp. 284–93 on justice between generations. See also Barry, pp. 189–212.

not because it has nothing to offer, but because it can be kept under control. Sufficient contribution can be exacted from members of the group without calling on their motives of fair reciprocity. Can the masters engage in fair reciprocity among themselves, cooperating to take from the helots by force? If so, what requirements of fair reciprocity are violated?

If an extant fair scheme of social cooperation includes everyone, then everyone is owed fair reciprocity. If helotry is already in force, though, it might be secure for the masters. What is needed is a helot group sharply identified by marks of birth, for in that case no master need fear exclusion. Rawls, of course, stoutly rejects any such exclusion—but where in a general rationale of Justice as Fair Reciprocity lie grounds for doing so?

III. Justice as Mutual Advantage

In the end Barry rejects Justice as Mutual Advantage, but first he gives it a lengthy run. Or at least he explores a closely related theory: that the requirements of justice are the ones that would be agreed to by ideal, self-interested bargainers. We might call this Justice as Ideal Bargaining Outcome. These two conceptions are not quite the same. Justice as Mutual Advantage assumes egoistic motives in society, and an egoist might not care about ideal bargains. He cares about actual bargains and what he can get away with. Egoistic bargaining does give rise to standards that suggest a kind of conventional justice, but ideal bargaining might settle on different standards from these.

Barry thinks there is sense in asking "what ideally rational bargainers would finish up with in any given situation" (p. 11). He needs to answer two classic objections to this claim. One stems from Thomas Schelling's work on bargaining: the outcome of actual bargaining, Schelling argued, depends greatly on the "salience" of some outcome for the bargainers— the subjective prominence of that outcome. That explains why the outcome is often to leave each "his own," and often to "split the difference." Salience lends itself poorly to fruitful idealization, and if we take salience away, nothing is left to determine the outcome of bargaining.[14] This objection Barry is at pains to answer.

14. Thomas Schelling, *The Strategy of Conflict* (Cambridge, Mass.: Harvard University Press, 1960), chap. 2.

The second objection is this: Concede that in two-person interactions, there is definiteness in how ideal bargaining would come out. Society, though, is not a two-person interaction. With more than two people, co-alitions come into play. What matters in multilateral bargaining is which coalition forms stably enough to dominate the others. That is partly a matter of historical happenstance. We cannot fruitfully ask what would happen with an ideal hypothetical bargain that abstracts away from the contingencies of history. Then, too, which coalition forms stably often depends on salient marks of group identity. If we want to know how so-cial bargaining will come out, it does no good to consult an ideal hypo-thetical bargain that abstracts away from such game-theoretic irrelevan-cies as skin color, dialect, kinship, dress, and ritual.

I myself think that both these objections are correct. In self-interested interactions, true enough, agents will often strike bargains and will often enforce them. That gives rise to actions that make it seem as if the agent is respecting conventional entitlements. (Of course, self-interested inter-actions also give rise to challenges, theft by stealth, raids, enslavement, and wars of attrition.) Now respecting entitlements can prevent wasteful struggle, and so bargaining to an agreement to respect a particular set of entitlements can be gainful for all. Once we have despaired of anything more inspiring, a strategy with great appeal is to find what is systematic in the waste-preventing aspects of egoistic interactions, and label it jus-tice.

This strategy depends on a claim that ideal hypothetical bargaining yields a definite outcome. Barry rebuts arguments that it will not. Justice as Ideal Bargaining Outcome is responsive to bargaining power. What exactly bargaining power means is unclear, but Barry thinks that we can find it in the abstract game-theoretic structure of two-person bargaining situations—and indeed that John Nash's famous solution captures ideal responsiveness to bargaining power. (Nash argued that bargainers will maximize the mathematical product of their utility gains—but exactly what his solution is will not matter for what I say here.) These claims raise many difficulties that Barry expounds marvelously, and I can only touch on what he says. Barry argues, first, that we have strong intuitions about bargaining power, and on this I think he is right. Barry thinks that the intuitions depend on the features of the situation captured by a stan-dard mathematical game theorist's analysis: the possible combinations of utilities the bargainers can jointly attain. I myself suspect that our intuitions on bargaining power are powerfully driven by factors that escape standard analyses—factors probably not capable of idealization.

Barry's clincher is a case of a rich man bargaining with a poor man over a pot of money. Neither will get anything unless they can agree on a division. The poor man is desperate for a small amount of the money in the pot, and needs the rest far less urgently (pp. 13–14). Now in this case, I agree, we do feel that the rich man is in the stronger position. The Nash solution, too, has the rich man coming away with the lion's share of the money, and so we might think that the Nash solution is vindicated.

Still, I claim, not all of the features that guide our intuitions of bargaining power help determine the Nash solution. Suppose instead that the poor man needs each dollar equally, and needs money desperately. Each five dollars will feed him another day. Suppose the rich man's pockets are empty, and he needs five dollars for a taxi ride in order to save himself a one-mile walk in gloomy weather. Any additional money he gets will go in the bank and be little noticed. Suppose they bargain over splitting one hundred dollars. In this case the Nash solution is to give most of the money to the poor man. Do we really think the poor man will have the lion's share of bargaining power?

Much of what makes for bargaining power is uncertainty. The rich man can act on a whim: he may feel magnanimous, or he may feel domineering. Quirks of mood affect his utilities, and so the poor man is uncertain what the rich man's utilities are. In economists' jargon, he is uncertain which divisions lie on the contract curve, the set of efficient divisions each prefers to disagreement. He does not know whether the rich man would rather spite him and walk in the rain rather than take less than the lion's share.

My own rough story of what goes on in self-interested bargaining would owe much to Schelling. Conventions latch onto subjectively prominent features of bargaining outcomes. Often, though, the conventional outcome turns out not to be mutually advantageous—or at least one party cannot be at all confident that it will be mutually advantageous. That may be because of personal quirks in utility, like mood, or, more probably, because of alternatives that each party can retreat to—self-reliance, or deals with third parties. When a convention becomes systematically disadvantageous to one kind of party—say, customary wages make for labor shortages, or a traditionally deferential caste gains economic power, or the ratio of young women to older men shifts—this puts pressure on the conventional outcomes. Novel accommodations are resented at first as unfair, but then they come to seem right and just.

In the end, as I say, Barry rejects Justice as Mutual Advantage. If I am right, though, he concedes more than he needs to along the way. Justice as Mutual Advantage is doubtfully captured by Justice as Ideal Bargaining Outcome, and Justice as Ideal Bargaining Outcome cannot be made coherent and convincing. Too much in actual bargaining depends on features of the situation that are not subject to standard game-theoretic idealizations.

IV. JUSTICE AS IMPARTIALITY

Barry's own conception of justice is Justice as Impartiality. In this volume, however, we learn more about what this conception is not than about what it is. Rawls (on one of his perches at least) tries to formulate such a conception by invoking his "original position," a hypothetical situation of self-interested negotiation from behind a veil of ignorance. In the original position, no one knows his own identity or various other facts about his situation, and each tries to do as well for himself as he can. Now Rawls thinks that behind this veil of ignorance, rational self-interested choosers would act with maximum risk aversion. They would choose the difference principle, to give those in the worst starting positions the best possible life prospects. Barry applauds the difference principle, but rejects Rawls's original position argument for the difference principle. He agrees with John Harsanyi's claim that the test of self-interest from behind the veil of ignorance yields utilitarianism. Barry mistrusts utilitarianism for much the same reasons as Rawls: chief among them, that utilitarianism, in some circumstance, might endorse outcomes like slavery that no one would find acceptable.

According to Barry, though, Rawls has another argument for the difference principle, to be found in chapter 2 of Rawls's book. This argument is valid, Barry says, and it "runs from equal opportunity to equality of income and from there to the difference principle via the notion of a Pareto improvement on equality" (p. 214). It is not supposed to be entirely distinct from the original position argument. The original position is meant only to represent "in a dramatic form the constraints that impartial appraisal imposes on anything that can count as a principle of justice" (p. 214). Barry takes it that the argument the original position dramatizes is supposed to be the equal opportunity argument of chapter 2. Barry thinks the arguments are in fact not equivalent, however, because the original position "does not capture adequately the moral insights that underlie Rawls's fundamental egalitarianism and drive his advocacy of the difference principle" (p. 215).

Rawls's argument in chapter 2 starts with a demand for equal opportunity. In a laissez-faire economy, three morally indifferent factors affect outcomes: natural talents, initial social circumstances, and subsequent luck. If we correct for a person's circumstances of birth and upbringing, we satisfy one demand of equal opportunity: that people with the same talent and ability and the same willingness to use them should have the same prospects for success. Then the only thing left to affect one's prospects at conception is genetic makeup. But genetic makeup is just as morally arbitrary as parental support and influence. A full-fledged demand for equality of opportunity would be that nothing morally arbitrary affect one's prospects—not even genetic makeup.

Still, if everyone's prospects can be improved by waiving the demand for this strict equality of opportunity, no one need complain of injustice. We move, then, to the social structure that makes the prospects of the worst-off group as good as possible. (There is more to be said about this move, and Barry scrutinizes it carefully, but this is roughly how it goes.) The chapter 2 argument, in short, pushes the rationale for equality of opportunity to the limit, and then allows a move to Pareto efficiency.

Rawls himself disclaims this as his official argument for the difference principle.[15] Still, Rawls does present the argument before disclaiming it, and, taken on its merits, the argument is well worth examining. Should we accept it? Should we demand equality of opportunity, and press this demand to the limit?

Justice does require equality in some sense: it requires, we might say, equality of consideration. But there are many ways this requirement could be interpreted. Utilitarianism offers one interpretation: everyone to count as one, and nobody as more than one. Utilitarianism treats everyone equally, in the sense that every person is told that his interests will be overridden only when otherwise others would have to forgo a greater interest. Why step, though, from this loose demand for equality of con-

---

15. Rawls, *A Theory of Justice*, p. 75.

sideration to the strict—and possibly expensive—demand that opportunities be equal? Or, more precisely, why demand that the least opportunities be as great as possible, cost what it may to achieve this? Increasing one person's prospects slightly, after all, may sometimes require decreasing another's greatly. A small increase in the prospects of the worst-situated may cost a big decrease in the prospects of the better-situated. Why must it be precisely this that justice demands?

Genetic makeup, social starting point, and luck are morally irrelevant. It might be claimed, then, that a social structure, to be just, cannot allow outcomes to depend on any of these properties. Strict equality would satisfy this demand, though equal prospects would not. (What could be of less moral relevance than pure luck?) A requirement of strict equality might be waived when it is to everyone's advantage to do so; this seems entirely reasonable. I argued above, however, that when a difference between people is morally irrelevant, what follows is not that this difference cannot be allowed to influence outcomes. What follows is that the social structure cannot be justified on the grounds that it makes outcomes depend on this property. If, though, the social structure can be justified in some other way, the fact that, under it, outcomes depend on morally irrelevant contingencies is no objection.

Barry has still another way to defend the difference principle—and this way will occupy the rest of the three-volume treatise. He calls his theory a form of *soft constructivism*. A theory is *constructivist*, he explains, if, first, it is a theory of pure procedural justice: "What comes out of a certain kind of situation is to count as just," and there is no standard of justice independent of this test (p. 266). Second, the test situation is hypothetical; it need not be played out in fact (as, say, a lottery must). The theorist posits the situation and deduces what would emerge from it. Barry's own constructivism is *soft* in that the parties have "a capacity and preparedness to be moved by moral considerations" (p. 350). They have human decency, with an emphasis on *human*.

Rawls, with his original position, sought a construction that would yield an outcome cleanly, without appeal to further moral notions. This hope Barry eschews; he does not think we can "hope for anything like a deductive proof" of which principles emerge from his framework (p. 345). We can ask, then, Barry recognizes, whether so soft a construction as his is doing any work. Barry's test is to ask which agreements agents of certain kinds could reject and still be reasonable. This puts the burden

on the moral term 'reasonable'. Barry does not think the term can use-
fully be defined; rather, we must depend on intuitive understandings.
Still, he thinks he can avoid simply "putting in as reasonableness what
we take out at the end as justice" (p. 347). The construction changes
one's ideas, he says: it "encourages—indeed, virtually forces—one to
make a distinction between what one would personally support and what
one believes could not reasonably be rejected" (p. 352).

In this first volume, Barry's discussion of these points is brief. Presumably we will learn more later. For now, we still need to ask how much a
soft construction can tell us. We do have intuitions, I agree, about what
is reasonable and what is not. The question is how we should regard
these intuitions. Perhaps they can be given an illuminating rationale.
Then we can see the intuitions as implicitly responding to this rationale.
If the rationale is good, we can regard the intuitions as giving us a kind
of knowledge of what is reasonable. We can hope, then, that Barry will
be able to display a convincing rationale for our intuitions that certain
principles could not reasonably be rejected.

If, though, the unreasonableness of rejecting certain principles is just
a brute moral fact, whispered to us by the voice of intuition, then I worry.
Argument stops somewhere, to be sure, but I hope it does not have to
stop with brute intuitions of what is reasonable and what is not. If someone tells me a demand is unreasonable, I want to ask why.

Subscription Rates

U.S. and Canada: individuals, 1 year $24.00, 2 years $48.00, 3 years $72.00; institutions, 1 year $40.00; students, 1 year $12.00; single issues, $8.00. Other countries add $9.25 per year for postage and handling for subscription orders, and $2.75 per issue for single issue orders.

To subscribe, write to Princeton University Press's distribution agent:
The Johns Hopkins University
  Press
Journals Division
701 West 40th Street, Suite 275
Baltimore, MD 21211 USA

Payments, inquiries, and all other correspondence relating to subscriptions should also be sent to The Johns Hopkins University Press.

Advertisements

Inquiries should be directed to
Journals Advertising Manager
Princeton University Press
41 William Street
Princeton, NJ 08540

Philosophy & Public Affairs acknowledges the assistance given to the Editor by the University of Southern California.

Philosophy & Public Affairs has been called "the leading journal in moral philosophy" by Peter Gibbins in *The Times Higher Education Supplement*.

Notes for Contributors

Contributions should be typewritten and double-spaced on standard-weight paper. Footnotes should also be double-spaced, numbered consecutively, and gathered at the end. Two clear photocopies should be submitted. Submissions will not be returned unless accompanied by a stamped, self-addressed envelope. Manuscripts and related correspondence should be directed to the Managing Editor, *Philosophy & Public Affairs*, Princeton University Press, 41 William Street, Princeton, NJ 08540.

Books for review and correspondence concerning the Review Section should be directed to Professor Charles Beitz, Department of Political Science, Swarthmore College, Swarthmore, PA 19081.

Philosophy & Public Affairs

Please order from Princeton University Press's distribution agent:
The Johns Hopkins University Press
Journals Division
701 West 40th Street, Suite 275
Baltimore, MD 21211 USA

Enter my subscription to **Philosophy & Public Affairs**

@ $_____ for _____ year(s).

Payment must be enclosed with order. Please do not send cash.

U.S. and Canada: *individuals*, 1 year $24.00, 2 years $48.00, 3 years $72.00; *institutions*, 1 year $40.00; *students*, 1 year $12.00. Other countries add $9.25 per year postage & handling.

Name _____

Address _____

City _____ State _____ Zip _____

Field or Discipline _____

Philosophy & Public Affairs

Please order from Princeton University Press's distribution agent:
The Johns Hopkins University Press
Journals Division
701 West 40th Street, Suite 275
Baltimore, MD 21211 USA

Enter my subscription to **Philosophy & Public Affairs**

@ $_____ for _____ year(s).

Payment must be enclosed with order. Please do not send cash.

U.S. and Canada: *individuals*, 1 year $24.00, 2 years $48.00, 3 years $72.00; *institutions*, 1 year $40.00; *students*, 1 year $12.00. Other countries add $9.25 per year postage & handling.

Name _____

Address _____

City _____ State _____ Zip _____

Field or Discipline _____

the review of
metaphysics

a philosophical quarterly

ISSN 0034-6632

JUNE 1991 | **VOL. XLIV, No. 4** | **ISSUE No. 176** | **$10.00**

articles

books received

philosophical abstracts

announcements

index

Individual Subscriptions $23.00   Institutional Subscriptions $40.00   Student/Retired Subscriptions $12.00

Jude P. Dougherty, Editor
The Catholic University of America, Washington, D.C. 20064

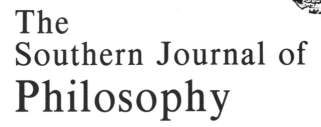

The
Southern Journal of
Philosophy

Spindel Conference proceedings only $10.00 each

Moral Epistemology - Vol. XXIX, 1990

Heidegger and Praxis - Vol. XXVIII, 1989

Aristotle's Ethics - Vol. XXVII, 1988

Connectionism - Vol. XXVI, 1987

B-Deduction - Vol. XXV, 1986

Moral Realism - Vol. XXIV, 1985

Recovering the Stoics - Vol. XXIII, 1984

Supervenience - Vol. XXII, 1983

Rationalist Conception of Consciousness - Vol. XXI, 1982

Planned for 1991 is a conference on
"Kant's Third Critique."

Proceedings published in the Spring following the conference.

For more information please write to:

THE SOUTHERN JOURNAL OF PHILOSOPHY
Department of Philosophy
Memphis State University
Memphis, Tennessee 38152
(901)678-2669

DIALOGUE

Canadian Philosophical Review/Revue canadienne de philosophie

Dialogue est la revue trimestrielle de l'Association canadienne de philosophie. Des contributions représentant les domaines principaux de la philosophie y sont publiées. Certains des articles du volume 28 sont mentionnés ci-dessous.

Dialogue is the quarterly journal of the Canadian Philosophical Association. Most of the main areas of philosophy are represented in its pages. Articles from Volume 28 are listed below.

Les manuscrits d'articles, d'études critiques et de comptes rendus rédigés en français ainsi que les livres pour recension doivent être adressés à: François Duchesneau, Département de philosophie, Université de Montréal, C.P. 6128, succ. A, Montréal, Québec, H3C 3J7, Canada.

English-language manuscripts and books for review should be sent to Professor Steven Davis, *Dialogue*, CC8311 Simon Fraser University, Burnaby, BC, V5A 1S6, Canada.

Les cotisations de membres (65 $; philosophes à la retraite, sans emploi ou détenant un emploi à temps partiel, 40 $; étudiants, 15 $) et les abonnements individuels à l'étranger (45 $) doivent être adressés à l'Association canadienne de philosophie, Pavillon Morisset, Université d'Ottawa, Ottawa, Ontario, K1N 6N5, Canada. Les abonnements institutionnels (au Canada, 60 $; à l'étranger, 65 $) doivent parvenir à Wilfrid Laurier University Press, Waterloo, Ontario, N2L 3C5, Canada.

Memberships ($65.00 regular; $40,00 retired, unemployed, and part-time philosophers; students $15.00) and foreign individual subscriptions ($45.00) should be addressed to the Canadian Philosophical Association, Morisset Hall, University of Ottawa, Ottawa, Ontario, K1N 6N5, Canada. Institutional subscriptions ($60.00 Canadian; $65.00 foreign) should be sent to Wilfrid Laurier University Press, Waterloo, Ontario, N2L 3C5, Canada.

The
Jerusalem
Philosophical
Quarterly

iyyun

Editor
EDDY M. ZEMACH
Managing Editor
EVA SHORR

NOW IN ENGLISH

Published in Hebrew since 1945 at the Hebrew University of Jerusalem, as of vol. 39 (1990) *Iyyun* appears four times a year: January (in English), April (in Hebrew), July (in English), October (in Hebrew). The English issues include summaries of the articles in the Hebrew issues.

Iyyun accepts long essays, articles, and critical studies irrespective of philosophical school or method of inquiry.

Forthcoming articles:

P.M.S. HACKER: R.L. Gregory's Theory of Perception
JAMES HIGGINBOTHAM: Truth and Understanding
KAI NIELSEN: Can there be Justified Philosophical Beliefs?
HARRY FRANKFURT: On the Usefulness of Final Ends

Recent articles:

CHARLES PARSONS: The Uniqueness of the Natural Numbers
WARREN GOLDFARB: Herbrand's Theorem and Incompleteness
MARK STEINER: The Autonomy of Mathematics
ITAMAR PITOWSKY: The Physical Church Thesis
ANTONY FLEW: Hume and Physical Necessity
MICHAEL DAVIS: The Market and Deserved Punishment
STAN GODLOVITCH: Music Performance and Tools of the Trade

Cheques should be made payable to the Jerusalem Philosophical Society and addressed to the S.H. Bergman Center for Philosophical Studies, The Hebrew University of Jerusalem, 91905 Israel.
Annual subscription: 4 issues $20 (postpaid $23); 2 (English) issues $10 (postpaid $12). Single issue: $7.

Cambridge University Press

The Political Responsibility of Intellectuals
Ian Maclean, Alan Montefiore, and Peter Winch, Editors
This book addresses the many problems in defining the relationship of intellectuals to the society in which they live. In what respects are they responsible for, and to, that society? Should they seek to act as independent arbiters of the values explicitly or implicitly espoused by those around them? Should they seek to advise those in public life about the way in which they should act, or should they withdraw from any form of political involvement? And how should their preoccupations with truth and language find practical expression?
39179-2   Hardcover $49.50
39859-2   Paper $15.95

The State and Justice
An Essay in Political Theory
Milton Fisk
"This is an important, ambitious book. Rather than continuing the debate about what Marx thought about justice or the state, Fisk has set out to construct a materialist theory of each, and their interrelation...He draws on concrete historical and contemporary experience to a degree rare among philosophers...Fisk is bold, unconventionial, provocative."
—David Schweickart,
Radical Philosophy Review of Books
37473-1   Hardcover $54.50
38966-6   Paper $18.95

Philosophy and Politics
G. M. K. Hunt, Editor
A volume of original works explores the relationship between the nature of man and the structure of society as part of a recurrent theme connecting philosophy and politics.
Royal Institute of Philosophy Supplements 26
39597-6   Paper $16.95

Moral Legislation
A Legal-Political Model for Indirect Consequentialist Reasoning
Conrad D. Johnson
This is a book about moral reasoning: how we actually reason and how we ought to reason. It defends a form of "rule" utilitarianism whereby we must sometimes judge and act in moral questions in accordance with generally accepted rules, so long as the existence of those rules is justified by the good they bring about.
Cambridge Studies in Philosophy
39224-1   Hardcover $39.50

Liability and Responsibility
Essays in Law and Morals
R. G. Frey and Christopher W. Morris, Editors
This collection of contemporary essays by a group of well-known philosophers and legal theorists covers various topics in the philosophy of law, focusing on issues concerning liability in contract, tort, and criminal law.
Cambridge Studies in Philosophy and Law
39216-0   Hardcover $54.50

Contractarianism and Rational Choice
Essays on David Gauthier's
Morals by Agreement
Peter Vallentyne, Editor
A number of prominent moral and political philosophers offer an assessment of Gauthier's theory—the most complete and suggestive contractarian theory of morality since the work of Rawls—and he responds in turn to their "critique."
39134-2   Hardcover $59.50
39815-0   Paper $19.95

Available in bookstores or write:
CAMBRIDGE UNIVERSITY PRESS
40 West 20th Street, New York, NY 10011-4211. Call toll-free 800-872-7423.
MasterCard/VISA accepted. Prices subject to change.